Tactics

Tactics

Rodney Pattisson

with Tim Davison
photographs by Tim Hore

Fernhurst Books

First published 1983 by
Fernhurst Books, 33 Grand Parade, Brighton, East Sussex BN2 2QA

British Library Cataloguing in Publication Data

Pattisson, Rodney
 Tactics. - 2Rev.ed. - (Sail to Win Series)
 I. Title II. Series
 623.8223

ISBN 0 906754 75 5

Acknowledgements

The publishers gratefully acknowledge permission to reproduce the
following photographs: pages 2, 29, 31, 56, 62 – Kos; pages 33, 41, 47 –
François Richard; page 35 – D. Edmund-Jones; pages 64, 67, 72, 83, 85 –
Roger Lean-Vercoe; page 89 – David Eberlin.
    Thanks are due to all those who helped with the photo sessions –
Richard Bates, Steve Blake, Philip Boutle, Clifford Crawshaw, Geoff
Crowther, Mark Griffiths, Martin Phillips, Richard Phillips and Rupert
Simpson. Thanks also to Queen Mary Sailing Club, Ashford, Middlesex
and Parkstone Yacht Club, Poole, Dorset for their hospitality during the
photo sessions.
    The cover design is by Behram Kapadia and the cover photograph is by
Kos.
    Diagrams by Pan Tek Arts, Maidstone and Chris Wood Design,
Titchfield.

Printed and bound in Great Britain

Composition by Allset, London & Central Southern Typesetters,
Eastbourne
Printed by Ebenezer Baylis & Son, Worcester

Contents

1 Tactical weapons

Sailing races are becoming harder and harder to win. Speed is essential, which means a properly tuned boat, sensitive technique, and an expert crew. But speed alone is useless if you point the boat in the wrong direction or collide with the opposition. So add to your shopping list good tactics, a sound knowledge of the rules and a tough mental attitude. Given all of these, and a bit of luck, winning becomes much easier!

In this book I concentrate on tactics — the art of making a race plan and then carrying it through, even in an international fleet.

First it's worth mentioning a couple of items invaluable for race decision-making.

Sight lines

Sight lines drawn on the deck are a useful aid to tactical thinking. Use the ones on the windward deck to help judge when to tack for the mark (figure 1). The sight lines on the leeward deck will indicate if you're on a collision course when beating and will help you judge when to gybe for the mark when tacking downwind. The angle required in each case is best found by experience. Bear in mind that the 'ideal' angles also change with conditions — in a Flying Dutchman, for example, we would gybe for the mark at 30° in strong winds, but at 80° in light winds — with the buoy almost abeam.

Compass

It is essential to have a compass on board — preferably one on each side deck. Choose the best you can afford — it should be large, with good lubber lines and clear numbers that can be read with the minimum of parallax. Before you buy a compass twist it in the shop to check that it's properly damped, and make sure it still swings freely when 'heeled'. Mount it on the boat where you can't help seeing it and clear of anything magnetic. Note that centreboards are often reinforced with steel rods, which will naturally affect the compass.

It's important to have the main lubber line pointing straight forwards so you can take bearings properly. To do this, first lay a string from the bow to the middle of the transom. Measure from the centre of the compass to this string — let's say the distance is 1 metre. Now measure 1 m out from the string at bow and transom and join these new points with a second string. Repeat the whole process for the compass on the other side, and then check that the two

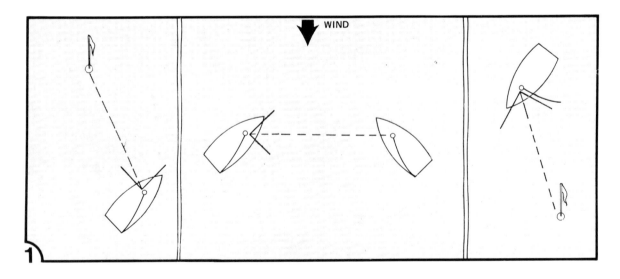

compasses give the same reading – if they don't, check for iron in their vicinity.

Wind and apparent wind

It is important at the outset to grasp the concept of apparent wind. There is much talk later in the book of keeping your wind clear, covering, blanketing and tide wind, which all refer to apparent wind; since this is the wind we use when racing let's discuss it here.

A boat at anchor feels the true wind. But a moving boat also feels a wind due to its own motion. If the boat is sailing at 3 knots over the ground, for example, she will be hit by 3 knots of motion wind straight on the nose (figure 2). In practice, of course, the crew feels only one wind, the result of adding the true wind and motion wind. This is called the apparent wind and can be calculated as in figure 3. Notice the apparent wind is stronger (5 knots) and from further ahead than the true wind. As the boat sails faster (say 4 knots) the apparent wind increases and moves still further forwards. The tide also contributes to the apparent wind, because it too moves a boat through the air. A boat becalmed bows-on to a 2-knot tide will feel a 2-knot tide wind from astern as she is swept backwards.

Although it helps to grasp all this, calculations afloat are not needed because the burgee shows the direction of the apparent wind. However, when you're making a race plan you would do well to bear these effects in mind, as I hope the following example will show.

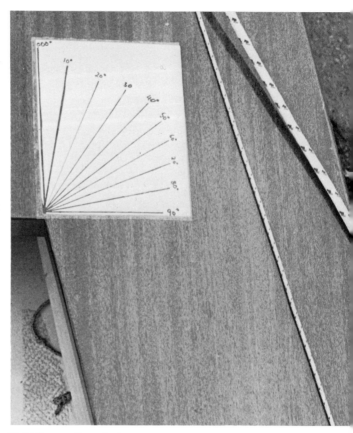

Sight lines on Superdocious.

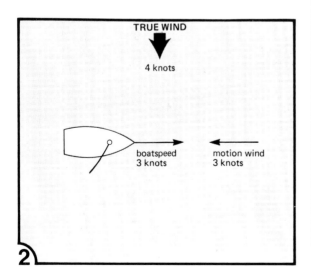

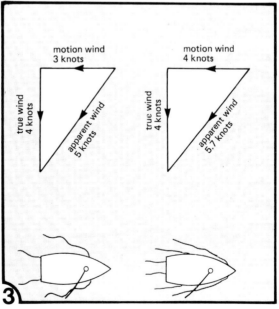

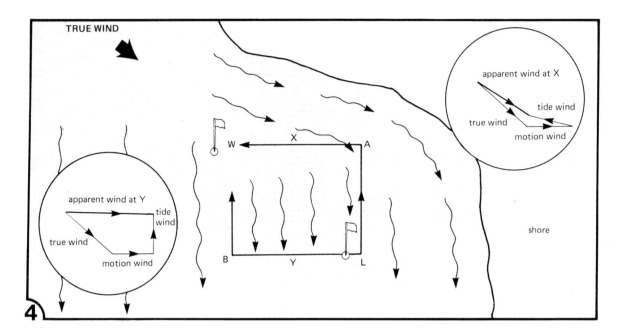

In Poole Bay, my home waters, the tide tends to follow the curve of the shore (figure 4). Even ignoring the differences in tidal strength across the course, it is much faster to take a long port hitch from the leeward mark and tack at A for the windward mark, W. This route gives you the tide almost dead ahead the whole way. The alternative route is a disaster, since the tide is setting you to leeward for the whole of leg LB, reducing the apparent wind *and* producing a header.

Attacking and defending with your sails

Figure 5 shows the areas of disturbed air around boats that are beating, reaching and running. These areas extend about five lengths to leeward in each case, but note that the beating boat also creates disturbed air one length to *windward* of its course. Other boats sailing in this disturbed air will be slowed. Boat B, however, is in the safe windward position relative to A — clear of her dirty air yet close enough to stop her tacking. Although the safe windward position usually doesn't stay safe for long, because A can either squeeze up or sail free to escape, it gives a useful short-term tactical advantage.

Using the wake

If you're not planing it's easy to get trapped in the quarter-wave of the boat ahead; but in marginal conditions, the quarter-waves can promote planing. To attack a boat ahead either stay outside the 'cone' of her wake altogether, or sail straight up behind and then luff across the quarter-wave. If the quarter-wave gets you planing, you have a chance of going through fast to weather.

You can also use the quarter-wave to hitch a 'tow' from a faster boat, by positioning yourself either to leeward or to windward. This can be amazingly effective, as I discovered on Magic Flamenco in one SORC race. In the middle of the night we hitched a ride on the quarter-wave of a larger, faster boat and were able to stay there on a broad reach for more than half an hour, steering by the light from her compass. Later in the series, though, we weren't so lucky — trying the same tactic on a run we broached and nearly eliminated both boats!

Practice

The only errors you should make are those forced on you by other boats. There is simply no excuse for fouling up through lack of practice — so sail, sail and sail again until everything works like clockwork. Then repeat the whole thing with another boat trying to wrong-foot you. Finally, race as often as you can — racing is the best practice of all and by far the most enjoyable.

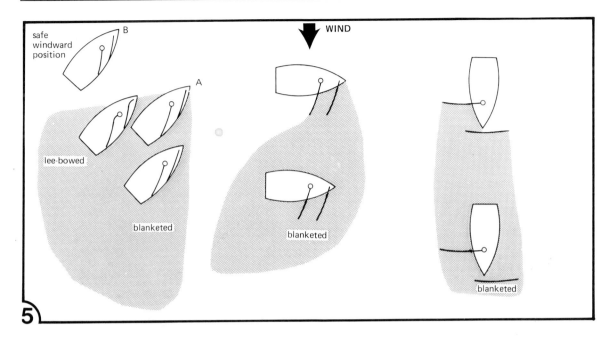

Above: here my Laser (102732) is in the safe windward position relative to 102536. Right: the windward Laser is just about to fall into her rival's lee bow and will soon drop back.

2 Shifts and bends

To work windshifts successfully, you must know the various types of windshift and be able to decide which type (or types) are affecting you on a particular day. The overall objective is to find a *pattern* to the shifts — and then take full advantage of it. There are three basic kinds of shift: oscillating shifts, permanent shifts and wind bends.

Oscillating shifts

These occur when the wind swings back and forth about a mean direction. A simple example would be where the wind swings right for 15 seconds, then left for 15 seconds and so on. Sometimes the shift cycle is much longer — between 5 and 30 minutes. These *phased shifts* are hard to detect before the start because of the time it takes to sort them out, but you can often spot the pattern during the race — particularly on the second beat.

Quite often you will detect the wind backing or veering with each gust. In this situation you can often anticipate the windshifts by looking for the gusts and lulls on the water ahead of you. If I *know* a header is coming I usually tack and am sheeted in again by the time the shift arrives, gaining valuable ground to windward.

Permanent shifts

A permanent shift takes place when the wind swings to one side and stays there.

On the morning of the race check the weather forecast to see if there will be a major permanent shift during the day. Try also to work out if a sea breeze will set in — if it does it will almost certainly cause a major windshift. If you think there will be a big permanent shift your only problem is one of timing — just when will it arrive? Usually I sail an unbiased race in these conditions, watching carefully for clear signs that the shift is about to arrive. As soon as I see that it's paying out to one side, and I think I know why, then I go that way. If you follow this advice you may lose one or two boats, but that's so much better than shooting the corners and risking a big loss.

Wind bends

A wind bend is quite different. It is usually caused by the wind bending around a solid object such as a hill on the shore. The bend will be there on every lap — it is far more reliable than the other types of shift. The rule with wind bends is always sail towards the centre of the bend: note how boat A in figure 1 gains

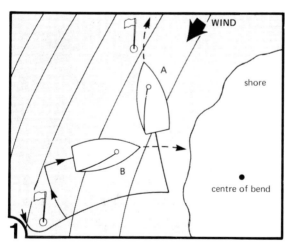

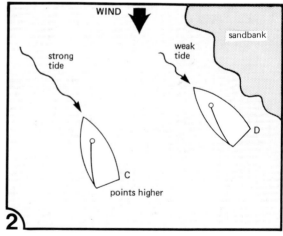

over boat B. The problem will be forcing yourself to sail into a header initially; it's only when you tack that you will reap your reward. Once again, understanding what's going on will give you the confidence to plough on in the early stages.

Sometimes a difference in tide wind across the course can cause an apparent wind bend. In figure 2, C is beating in strong tide so is moving slowly over the ground. D is in weaker tide so is making more headway. The result is that C will point higher – giving D's helmsman a worrying time unless he realises what's going on.

An offshore wind usually bends as it meets the sea. Again, you should sail towards the centre of the bend.

On the water

One of your first jobs on the water is to find out what the shifts are actually doing, and this is where your compass comes into its own. Begin beating on starboard and sail for as long as possible on that tack, reading the compass every few seconds. What is the mean reading? How much does the reading change to each side of this mean? How often does a large shift

Before the start beat for a while on each tack to check the compass bearings.

(more than 5°) take place? Now tack and repeat the process on port. At the end of your pre-start exercise you should have a mental picture of the shifts, e.g. "The shifts are oscillating about once a minute. The mean reading on starboard is 135°. A good lift is about 145°. A bad header is about 125°. So I'll tack if it's less than 130°. The mean reading on port is . . .". If you find the figures hard to remember, write them down on the deck with a chinagraph pencil.

If you're worried about getting back to the start (because of a strong tide, or because you don't have much time) you can take a series of true wind readings instead (see chapter 3). This will certainly tell you how the shifts are behaving, but you miss out on the reassurance of knowing the starboard and port tack bearings.

All this information must be integrated with your race strategy. If the shifts are oscillating and there are no other factors, you'll want to stay near the middle of the beat and tack on shifts. Don't sail near the lay lines or you may be caught out by a shift – there's nothing worse than wanting to tack on a shift but knowing that to do so would take you over the lay line (you would then be overstanding the mark). So play the shifts as soon as possible after the start; in an evenly matched fleet it is the only way to pull ahead.

3 Checking the course

Mark bearings

The committee usually displays the bearing of the first mark. Although this is a useful aid to spotting the windward mark, the bearing itself is useless because it's the reading from the leeward mark to the windward mark you'll use during the race.

So, either on the run out to the start or during your pre-start tuning, sail up to the leeward mark. Align your boat with the leeward and windward marks and take a bearing. Write it down, then use it to calculate the expected bearings of the other legs. In the example below I am assuming the usual 45° Olympic course (figure 1).

Example:

> *Bearing of windward mark = 260°*
> *Run = 80° (260° − 180°)*
> *First reach = 125° (run + 45°)*
> *Second reach = 35° (run − 45° OR*
> *   run + 360° − 45°)*

Knowing these bearings gives you confidence on large courses. On the reach sail on the bearing until you can see the next mark. On the run bear away onto the calculated bearing, then decide which gybe you should

be on. On later beats the bearing of the windward mark helps you to orientate yourself after major windshifts especially in bad visibility. You may even be able to sail directly to the windward mark if the windshift was large.

Having sorted out the course, the next job is to check the start line. Indeed the secret of a good start lies in the preparatory work you do, the most vital factors being finding a transit, and assessing the bias of the line.

Transits

Since your aim is to be just behind the line at the start, you must know where the line is. A *transit* will tell you your exact position relative to the line.

Just before the ten-minute gun, and when you're sure the committee won't alter the line, sail up to the committee boat and line up its mast (or whatever is prescribed in the racing instructions) with the pin. Look for another object in the line — a moored boat, or a building on the shore would be ideal (figure 2). Sometimes you may have to stand to see over the committee boat and you may even have to position yourself on the line side of it. Later, when you're preparing to start, you can inch forwards until the object

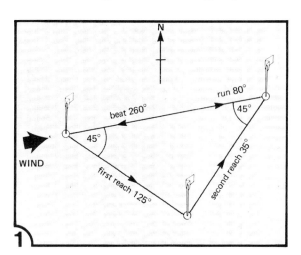

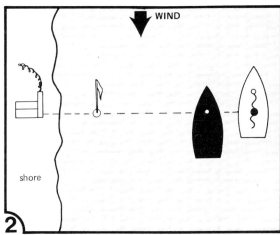

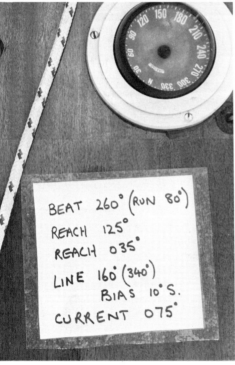

BEAT 260° (RUN 80°)
REACH 125°
REACH 035°
LINE 160° (340°)
        BIAS 10° S.
CURRENT 075°

Top: the 'tiller method' of assessing your position relative to the line. Right: checking the start-line bias. I am taking a transit and will use it to sail along the line with the luff just lifting (see next page). My crew meanwhile reads the bearing of the line. Above: the data gathered in this chapter are recorded like this. I've also added the direction of the current.

and pin are in line again. Any further, and you'll be over.

A common mistake in using this method is to forget that when your eye is on the line, your bow is well over! So allow a safety margin of, say, 3 m in a Laser, 5 m in a Dutchman and nearly 7 m in a Soling.

If there is no convenient object (or no shore in this direction!) attempt a transit from the pin end. This method is equally accurate but gives you the problem of having to look constantly over your shoulder as you line up to start.

Sometimes it is not possible to fix a transit from either end. In this case use the 'tiller method' to check when you're on the line. Simply sail along what you believe is the line, centralise the tiller and sight back along it towards the mast of the committee boat (or the pin). If your line of sight is behind the committee boat, you're probably OK – if not, you're over.

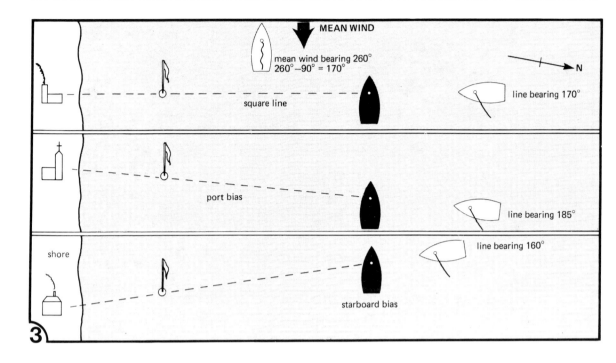

A further problem crops up when the line is very long and the committee moves it just before (or even after!) the five-minute gun. There is no time to sail to an end to take a new transit — so use the tiller method instead to position yourself on the line, and sight through the committee boat (or pin) to get the transit.

The tiller trick is also a useful way of checking, seconds before the gun, if your transit has altered — particularly if the rest of the fleet seems to be hanging back. But beware the one-minute rule here, and also make sure you don't have a competitor close to leeward preventing your swinging round.

Line bias

Your next step is to check the angle of the start line to the wind. Usually, one end is further to windward and you will want to start at or near that end. I'll describe two methods of doing this.

To find the bias without using a compass, use your transit to help you sail along the line on port tack, adjusting the mainsheet so the luff just flaps. Cleat the sheet (or hold it in the same position), tack and sail back down the line. If the luff just flaps, the line is square. If the sail flaps more, start near the port end of the line; if the sail flaps less (or you have to let

it out to make it flap) start near the starboard end.

At the end of your line check, luff to closehauled to make sure the wind is in its mean direction. If not, repeat your check until you are confident of your findings. This method is most accurate if you are in the middle of the line and there is little current running. I like to keep the mainsheet cleated at the 'just flapping' position throughout my pre-start manoeuvres so I can point the boat along the line at any time to check the line bias.

Alternatively, find the bias using the compass as follows.

1 Use your transit to help you take a compass bearing of the line. Write it down, and also the reciprocal (see example below).
2 Find the true wind direction by going head to wind. Wait until you are almost stopped with the boom central and the windex dead fore-and-aft before asking your crew to take the reading.
3 Subtract 90° from the true wind reading.

If bearings (3) and (1) coincide, the line is square. If (3) is larger than (1), start near the *starboard* end. If (3) is smaller than (1), start near the *port* end. All this is summed up in figure 3. It is as well to check the true wind and repeat the calculation several times in case the wind is oscillating.

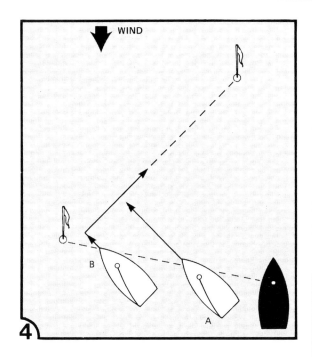

Example:

(1) *Line bearing 160° (reciprocal 340°)*

(2) *True wind 260°*

(3) *True wind bearing − 90° = 170°*

Bearing (3) exceeds (1), so the starboard end is favoured.

Windward mark position

The methods above assess the start line relative to the wind. Unless you can actually lay the mark from one end of the line, the position of the windward mark is

Taking a true wind reading. With the boom central and the boat head to wind, I check the windex while the crew takes the reading. Below: a reliable transit is essential for starting in the middle of a long start line.

completely irrelevant. You might, for example, think that the starboard end would be best in figure 4 because it is nearer the windward mark; but B sails a shorter distance than A because she has realised that the pin end was further to windward.

Once you know which end of the line to start and how far you are from the line, you can decide on your starting strategy.

4 Starting on a port-biased line

Even in top events you can get a violently biased line. In the first race of the 1968 Olympics the port end was so favoured we could hardly lay the line on starboard tack. The 35-odd Dutchmen all went for the best start and piled into one another — although we eventually extricated ourselves and won the race we were disqualified later in the protest room. Not a very good way to start an Olympic series! The start of the last race was an action replay of the first — except for one boat (ours!) deliberately manoeuvring at the wrong end of the line. From such a cautious start we could only finish second in the race, but that was enough to take the gold medal overall.

This story helps point out the dangers of a port-end start. In fact I never start right by the pin now, preferring to line up *towards* the pin end just clear of the bunch. I'm even more cautious if I've already had my discard, when I'd start further towards the middle and try to use speed to pull through. On the other hand I *would* go for the best start on a starboard-biased line (see chapter 6) because it's then much easier to find a gap.

Before looking at port-end starts in depth, let's first see what can go wrong.

Port-end dangers

The nastiest feeling is that experienced by the 'pin-end pusher'. In his enthusiasm to be right by the buoy at gunfire, he arrives too early. The only possibilities left are to hit the buoy, push over the line too early or to duck behind the line. All are disastrous! It is only slightly less unfortunate to get stuck in a raft of early boats — like black in figure 1. Even if you make an apparently good start you'll find it hard to clear the bunch, and with a line of boats on starboard coming up behind you, you can't tack clear. Sometimes the pin is a boat; then you have to leave enough room to clear it and its anchor line. In figure 2 the shaded area must be avoided; there are usually committee members on the boat, too, so your chances of getting away with an infringement are slight!

Port-end advantages

Despite all this, if you find the line biased to port there are good reasons for starting near the favoured end. Many people have a horror of starting at the port end — you can't hear the countdown on the committee boat (they think) and if things go wrong you've

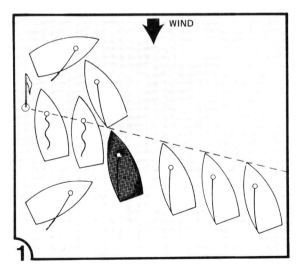

1

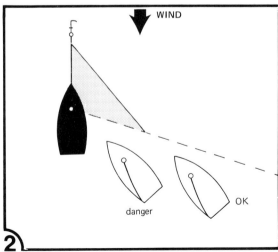

2

got to go behind the whole fleet. So what are the advantages of starting at the port end?

The most obvious advantage is distance to windward. A boat at the pin end of a port-biased line could easily be 4 boat-lengths further to windward than a boat at the starboard end, and that distance at the start often means the difference between first and last.

Secondly, a port-end start means there are no boats to leeward so you can sail at full speed. Even if a windward boat starts coming over the top of you, you can bear away, accelerate and keep your wind clear.

The third advantage is psychological – a good start by the pin gives a warm glow and a pump of adrenalin just when it's needed. If you're good enough to win the start, why not the race?

Lastly, if you want to sail to the left of the course it makes sense to start near the port end of the line.

Having decided to start near the port end, the method of achieving that aim depends on the type of boat you're sailing.

Port-end starting technique

Technique in boats that tack quickly. Keep near the pin so that you are right by it on port tack with one minute to go. Have a look at the other competitors lining up to start. A typical situation is shown in figure 3, where boat A is too early, B probably about right and C too far back. Simply reach behind A and tack just to leeward of B. There's ten seconds to go,

In this Fireball fleet K-8827 makes the perfect pin-end start.

you have more way on than the boats around you and you're right by the pin, so just sheet in and go!

Often, the whole fleet is hanging back too far. In this case, sail up to the first boat and tack on her lee bow (as you did to B). You must now protect the large 'hole' between you and the pin. If someone looks like reaching through you to leeward, raise the centreboard and drift sideways. Otherwise, hang back until there are 15 seconds to go, then reach for the pin so you cross the line with full speed.

Technique in boats that tack slowly. In a larger boat you can use the same sort of technique to get into position. Sail in on port and tack so that you're lined up with one minute still to go. You should be slightly to windward of where you want to start, and squeezing up to make a hole to leeward (it's too late for anyone to fill this hole). When you're ready power off into the hole and over the line.

What next?

Having made a good start, the temptation is to sail on enjoying the discomfort of those around you. Try to resist this. Remember, you may be temporarily in the

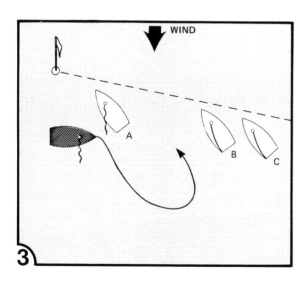

3

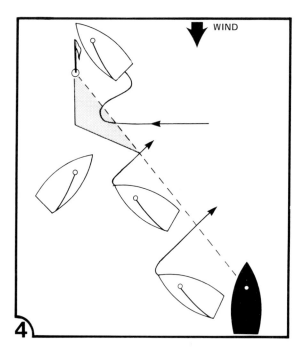

4

WIND

lead but you're out on a limb. As soon as you're sure you can clear the boats on starboard, tack onto port and consolidate your advantage. When you're to windward of the centre of the fleet, tack back onto starboard again — now you're ahead, in touch with both wings and fully in control.

A really biased line

Sometimes the line is so biased that you can't even *lay* it on starboard tack. In this case there's an odd area by the buoy that can't be reached by a conventional starboard-tack approach (figure 4). You can take advantage of this either by starting on port tack in the shaded area, or (if there's no one-minute rule) by scooting into it on starboard from above the line. Make sure you're behind the line as the gun goes, then luff past the pin and off into the lead.

Remember — to get a large fleet away, most committees bias the line to favour the pin end. So learning to get away from near the port end is a vital part of your starting armoury.

5 Starting mid-line

In the middle of the line there are no constrictions, so you can expect a bit of room to make a good start. If you want to win a particular race you need to go for the *best* start; but in a series you can't afford to put yourself at risk so starting away from the ends makes sense. And if you have good boatspeed, why risk a start-line incident?

When should you start mid-line?

1 When there are good transit facilities. The problem with the mid-line start is knowing where you are on the line. The longer the line the worse the problem. A transit is the best solution. But if you can't get a

transit you can sometimes point the bow at the pin, centralise the tiller and sight backwards towards the committee boat, as described in chapter 3.

One of the best starts I ever made was in Kiel Week in a fleet of 80 Dutchmen. The funnel of the committee boat lined up with a lump on a hill on the shore; it was a difficult transit to spot and, moreover, the current was setting the fleet back from the line. In the middle there was a huge bulge back. I waited in line with the others until 30 seconds before the start — not wanting to give the game away — then sheeted in early and moved forwards several lengths into clear air. At gunfire we had the satisfying sight of a line of boats well to leeward; although a recall gun was fired that transit gave us the confidence to carry on and win the race, despite discouraging comments from our nearest rivals right to the finish!

2 When there is no bias on the line and no tidal advantage at either end. By starting in the middle you lose nothing and have the flexibility to go either way if one side begins to pay.

3 If there is a port bias to the line but the tide favours the right of the course. Starting at the port end is risky because you have to cross the whole fleet to get right. Starting in the middle is a good compromise. The same tactic pays off when there is no tide but the shore is to the right. As we saw in chapter 2, it pays to take advantage of the wind bend by going inshore.

4 If one end is favoured and causing excessive bunching. In this case start clear of the bunch towards the middle of the line.

5 If you want to play safe. If you have good boatspeed or if you're leading on points, start in the middle.

6 In a foul current. There is almost always a bulge back in the line caused by boats bunching, flapping

Laser 100302 (arrowed) makes a good start by slowing and luffing to open a large gap to leeward. The boat behind starts to reach into the hole but 100302 sees her coming, lets out her boom and gathers speed to make an excellent start with no one close to leeward.

and getting pushed back by the tide. In the middle you can gain most advantage over neighbouring boats.

7 In shifty winds — when you want to go up the middle of the course.

Don't start mid-line . . .

1 If there's a round-the-ends rule. If you're pushed over the line you'll never make it to one end — your race is over!

2 If the current is with you. It's very difficult to judge if you're being pushed over. You may also be surrounded by idiots who are miles past the line — although they'll be disqualified later they will still take your wind and ruin your start, and may even have dragged you over with them!

Starting in a dinghy

With two minutes to go you should be on port, slightly behind the line that's beginning to form. As late as you dare, tack into the windward end of a hole and slow down by pushing out the boom. Don't stop completely or you'll drift down and close the hole. Try to keep your bow level with the boats to windward — don't let them get ahead. If someone there pulls his sheets in too early, shout to encourage him to stay back. Most important of all is to try to keep two or three boat-lengths away from the boat to leeward. In practice this is hard to do — you may have

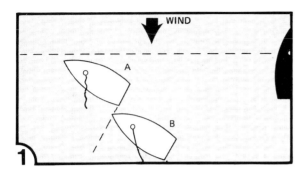

to settle for one and a half lengths. This distance is far more important than fore-and-aft advantage — though that's nice too!

If the boat to leeward reaches off he will open up such a large gap that other helmsmen will be tempted to fill it. In this case reach off with him, keeping the gap between you constant. But if the competitor to leeward stays put, remember at the start to pull in your sails *travelling straight ahead*. If you have one and a half lengths between you the boat to leeward will have to point so high to interfere with you that you'll go over the top of him, but you'll never achieve this if you close up the gap just before the gun. In a Dutchman we pull in both sails together with about 15 seconds to go. As we sheet in the crew goes out on the trapeze. The timing will vary from class to class and keelboats obviously need more time, but the objective is the same — full speed at the gun.

If someone looks as though he's going to tack to leeward of you just before the start, let out your sheets and bear off as you see him coming. This may persuade him to go to windward, or to look for another hole. But if he does come in to leeward the speed you've gained is useful — you can luff hard and open some distance between you. Remember you don't have to respond to his cries of "up, up" until he gains an overlap — and then he must give you room to keep

clear. Figure 1 shows the point at which A must *start* keeping clear of B.

Alternatively, if you have room to weather you can put in two short tacks to re-establish your hole. If you find that people often attack you in this way, you're probably making too big a hole to leeward — try being content with something smaller!

As you become more proficient, you may find you pick up a group of 'camp followers' who try to start alongside you. The only way to avoid them is to line up in the wrong place, then reach off at the last minute to the right spot and find a hole. This works best if the current is running against you.

Starting in a keelboat

The main aim in a keelboat is to have boatspeed at the gun. You should also have a hole to leeward. Since it takes at least 30 seconds to get a keelboat going, the boats need to line up some way back from the start line and rather earlier than for a dinghy start.

With one minute to go you want to be in position, several lengths back from the line. You can attain this position either by approaching the line of boats on port tack and tacking into a hole with just over a minute to go, or alternatively by lining up early and squeezing up to windward to make a hole for yourself. The hole is less likely to get filled than with a dinghy start, because the windshadow from a keelboat is large — other boats thus find it difficult to reach beneath you and luff into your hole. Incidentally, watch out for your mast during the pre-start manoeuvres: as the boat to leeward luffs her mast will come upright and may strike yours if you're heeling.

With 45 seconds to go everyone tends to bear away to pick up speed. Since it's essential for you to keep in line with (or ahead of) the others you must watch the boats to leeward carefully so you can bear away as soon as they do. Only hang back if you're sure the others are going to be early, and that no-one will get a lee-bow position on you.

Below: coming in late on port, 77946 tacks into a hole on the line for a good, opportunist start.

6 Starting on a starboard-biased line

A good race officer always tries to give the line a slight port bias; so if the line is biased to starboard the committee is probably suspect — you will either have recall after recall or they'll let the fleet go despite several boats being over. Either way, you've got to get off that line cleanly.

The inner distance mark

The committee often lays a small buoy on or near the line. This is the inner distance mark (IDM) and you're not allowed to pass between it and the committee boat. The purpose of it is not only to prevent competitors chipping the committee boat's paint, but also to give the OOD a chance to see down the line — otherwise one sail right beside him might completely obscure the start.

Usually, the IDM is positioned just *over* the line. Occasionally it is right *on* the line. If it is *behind* the line, check the sailing instructions carefully — sometimes you can sail round the IDM on the required side and then move towards the committee boat, while keeping behind the line (figure 1). You can get a fantastic start like this. But often the instructions specifically forbid passing between the IDM and committee boat — so beware!

Starboard-end dangers

The biggest danger is of being squeezed out. The right-hand boat in figure 2 has no rights over black who can push her the wrong side of the IDM.

If you're the type who likes to get away with murder at the start, don't do it at the starboard end. You're right in front of the OOD who should spot any infringement.

If the line is really biased to starboard, there'll be a bunch at the end of the line and you may get stuck in it. Even worse, you may get hit by a rogue reacher who zooms down the line with no rights. It's no consolation being in the right when the idiot capsizes on top of you or even puts a hole in your side. Your only chance is to keep an eye open to windward and to shout loud and early if the boats to windward decide to reach towards you.

Starboard-end advantages

If the line is biased to starboard you gain ground to windward by starting near the windward end.

If you plan to go towards the right of the course, a starboard-end start is essential. After the gun you can tack onto port and go the way you want. If you start

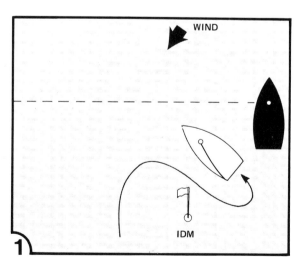

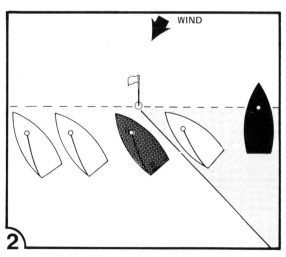

at the port end, you'll have to battle across the whole fleet to get to the right-hand side.

Starboard-end starting technique

Let's suppose the line is biased 5° to starboard, and the IDM is on the line. If you want to be sure of getting away with a *reasonable* start, try to be a third of the way down the line when the gun goes. In these circumstances, though, I'd probably try for the *best* start – in other words to be right by the IDM at the gun. Boatspeed is not too important – in fact it's impossible to get a run at the line because of the crowded conditions. If you do get lee-bowed after the start you can always tack off, and nothing is lost.

Ideally you want to be two lengths from the IDM with a minute to go, and then move forwards close-hauled as slowly as possible so you arrive at the IDM at the start. Boats to windward are squeezed out, while boats to leeward can't touch you since you're already sailing as close to the wind as you can.

So how do you get into that position two lengths from the line? You can't afford to sail in from too far back, or you'll find a wall of boats ahead of you.

OK, so they're too early – but you still can't sail through them. One method is to come in high, raise your centreboard and drift down into position. Another is to sail in slowly on a closehauled course. If you try this *don't* come in from too far back, and *do* try a few dummy runs; you may even be able to get a bearing or a back-bearing, which will help on your actual approach. However, your wind will be much less clear just before the start, so come in a little higher than the dummy run suggests.

All this is simple to say, but hard to put into practice. If you find yourself *above* the ideal course raise your centreboard early and drift down. Alternatively, you can tack off and try again – if you have time. If you find yourself to *leeward* of the ideal course, you may be able to put in a quick tack to get across to it. If you're *late* – don't panic. Wait until the front rank starts, then tack as soon as you can clear the committee boat. The boats ahead can't tack in your water, and you should find yourself hammering off into clear air on port.

If you're very early you've got real problems. Try to realise your mistake in good time and stop by pushing your boom out. If you're really early and there's

no one-minute rule, reach down to find a hole. Alternatively if the committee boat is small, circle round it and try again.

Allowing for the tide

If the tide is setting down the line towards the pin, there will always be a hole by the IDM on the first start (on later starts everyone will have realised what's going on). Helmsmen only have to let their sails flap for a few seconds to be swept down the line. The same is true if you're starting against the tide: since the boats are at an angle to the current they still get pushed away from the IDM. In either of these circumstances it's worth trying to reach in around the IDM for the pole start.

Left: This start is against the tide. Knowing that the early starters will be set down from the IDM, I choose to come in very high, raise my centreboard and slide into the pole position. Above: Laser 2's bunching at the starboard end.

If the tide is setting along the line towards the committee boat, or pushing the fleet over the line, start well away from the starboard end.

Starting with no IDM

If there's no IDM the above advice still applies, but you also have a nice little 'corner' by the committee boat to luff into for an extra-special start. If you do so, allow time for getting through the windshadow of the committee boat — it's not much fun sitting there with your sails flapping while the fleet disappears into the distance.

What next?

Unless the right-hand side is very favoured, sail on for a while on starboard tack. This gets you back in touch with the middle of the fleet; once in the centre you can control things better. However if you get headed badly you must tack or risk all the boats to leeward of you crossing ahead.

7 The gate start

Everyone has the chance to make a perfect gate start. Top sailors dislike the gate for just this reason — with a line start they can safely assume at least half the fleet will start badly in dirty wind. But with a gate start everyone surges forward in clear air, and the first leg becomes purely a boatspeed contest. Indeed if the weather mark is too near, the whole fleet may arrive in a bunch. Despite these problems, the gate start is a common way of getting a big fleet away, so your success in a championship may hinge on your skill with the gate.

Deciding when to start

Check the tide and windshifts before the ten-minute gun as described in chapter 2. Also assess the speed of the pathfinder *in today's conditions*. These three factors will influence your decision on where to start through the gate.

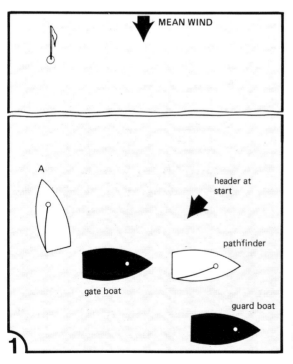

MEAN WIND

A

header at start

pathfinder

gate boat

guard boat

1

Reasons for starting early

1 If the pathfinder is slow. There is no point in waiting for several minutes while the pathfinder dawdles across the fleet.

2 If there are few windshifts and the pathfinder is slow. In the absence of shifts it's normally difficult to tack onto port and sail across the fleet. However, if the pathfinder is slow she will hold the fleet back enough for you to get across.

3 If there are frequent windshifts. If you start early you can be tacking on the shifts while the pathfinder is plugging along on port tack. In any case, you will need a header at some stage to get you back across the fleet!

4 If the wind cycle indicates the pathfinder will be starting out on a header. In this case you'd be starting on a lift — nice work if you can get it! Note in figure 1 how this (somewhat exaggerated) header results in the pathfinder making no progress towards the windward mark, while the early starters (like A) are almost sailing straight to it. I'll describe how to check the wind cycle later in this chapter.

5 If there is a tidal advantage to the left of the course.

Reasons for starting late

1 If the pathfinder is fast.

2 If you're slow!

3 If the wind cycle indicates the pathfinder will be starting out on a lift.

4 If there is a tidal advantage to the right of the course. As an example, it might pay to make short tacks up the right-hand side of the course, because the tide is slacker there. An early start would mean you have to cross the whole fleet to reach the right side — something few early starters will manage!

Opposite: opening the gate. The pathfinder, preceded by the guard boat, sets off on port tack while the Enterprise fleet waits with sails flapping.

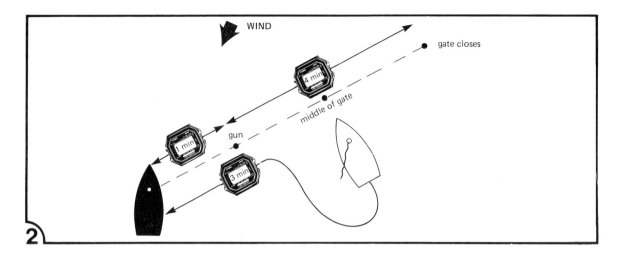

Reasons for starting in the middle

1 Pathfinder's speed is fair.

2 Shifty conditions.

3 Fleet bunching at either end.

Gate starting technique

Let's assume that the pathfinder will sail for one minute before the start, then for a further four minutes to open the gate. These are quite common time periods. Unless you're certain which end of the gate to start, you should be in the middle of the gate at the five-minute gun. If you find it hard to judge this, begin by sailing closehauled on port from the committee boat with eight minutes to go, and carry on for three minutes. You're now roughly in the middle of the gate, with five minutes left (figure 2). Tack onto starboard and check your compass: are you on a lift or a header? It would be nice to continue checking the wind until near the start — but realistically you're not going to be able to do it much later than the five-minute gun.

Now, using your pre-start analysis of the windshifts, try to predict if the pathfinder will be starting on a header or a lift. If you reckon she'll be starting on a header, you've just got time to reach down and start early (see below). If not, stay put or tack onto port and start late.

While you're waiting for the pathfinder, keep well to windward — five lengths to leeward of the pathfinder's course is ideal. This is so you can manoeuvre, which is impossible if your wind is cut off by other boats. Now is the time to watch for bunching, and

begin by moving towards a clear part of the gate. Avoid lining up to windward of someone fast or (worse) someone who points higher than you, as they'll cause you great problems just after you start. All the while keep an eye on the pathfinder; if she's headed, reach flat out to make as early a start as you can manage.

Having chosen your spot, make a hole to leeward by letting your sails flap and by luffing slightly. The idea is to hold back the boats to windward — though you must watch to make sure no one reaches over the top of you. If you see someone coming — shout! The chances are she'll hit the gate boat and/or you, and very likely ruin your start. If she keeps coming your only option is to sheet in and go too.

One word of warning: don't make too big a hole to leeward or someone else will fill it! It wants to be just big enough to keep you well clear of the boat to leeward — anything more is an open invitation to the late starters.

As the guard boat approaches, assess if it is on station. Often it is too far back, which means you can't lay the gate boat's stern after going round the guard boat. If this is the case, sail flat out for the stern of the guard boat right away. If the guard boat is too far forward, ignore it and go for the gate boat's stern. Remember — a steady bearing on its transom indicates you're on course. Don't reach in but sail a fast, slightly free windward course. Only if there's a huge hole to leeward can you allow yourself to close reach for extra speed; but even then you tend to lose ground to windward as you turn round the gate boat. Normally it's very difficult to hit the gate boat — its wash seems to push you back as you approach. So aim slightly forward of its transom with your crew trapezing in a hunched position so you can round really close.

How to start early

Trying to start first through the gate is very risky because it's almost impossible to judge where the (moving) gate boat will be at the starting gun. If you do decide to start first you'll need to do a dummy run from the committee boat, sailing on port for one minute to help you guess where the free-floating buoy will be dropped. If you notice some top helmsmen doing the same, abandon your idea — there's only room for one boat to start first and if it's not you, you may as well go home!

The technique is similar to that described above. Reach down until you get to a position you're happy with, about four to five lengths below the pathfinder line. Sit and flap, gradually making a gap to leeward and watching to weather for boats reaching in. Ease forwards, then beat flat out for the gate boat.

After the start

If you have a problem with the boat to leeward, your preparation was at fault — either you didn't make a hole or you reached in to the gate. You must stay away from the boat to leeward, preferably by sailing fast but *in extremis* by pinching. If it all goes wrong, wait for a shift and tack. If no shift comes, tack onto port anyway and (if necessary) sail behind the whole fleet out to the right of the course. You will only lose a couple of boats lengths doing this — far less than if you'd carried on in dirty air (see also chapter 8).

If your start is good, sail on starboard until you get a header, then tack. If you have someone to windward, shout to persuade her to tack first. If she carries on, bear away a bit and tack behind her. But don't tack until you're sure you can clear most of the fleet; if you have to duck more than half a dozen transoms on your way across, you'll find yourself ducking the whole fleet — in the meantime you're out on a limb, and vulnerable. So watch for that shift!

8 Recovering from a bad start

Since only a few boats can get a good start, it follows that most of the fleet will start badly. Thus the ability to recover is one of the most vital skills in a sailor's armoury. Quick, remedial action is needed, both to prevent further loss of distance and to bolster your sagging confidence.

Recovering from a bad line start

The most common problem from a line start is being lee-bowed. If you're only just entering the lee-bow zone (and there's no one close to windward) it's worth squeezing up to try to escape. This works well in a keelboat, but in smaller classes pinching slows the

boat and gives less lift from the centreboard, resulting in your drifting sideways deeper into the lee-bow. If squeezing doesn't work tack onto port, duck a few transoms and look for a hole to tack back into. The only time you should stay on starboard and take your medicine is when you *know* that starboard is the only tack to be on.

Sometimes the boat to windward of you hits the line fast and begins to drive over you. Firstly, remember that the opposition is not technically allowed to bear down on you, so shout if she appears to be doing so! If this fails you can try bearing off to gain speed, although you obviously need a gap to leeward. This works well in boats like the Dutchman where freeing

Freeing off to escape 91123's windshadow works well for this Laser because she has space to leeward.

off results in a large gain in speed — but remember that you *are* losing ground to windward and this can cost many boats. Once again, if you're badly trapped your only escape is to tack onto port and try to get clear that way.

Over the line

If you're well over the line — come back. There's little point in carrying on and being disqualified. If you have good boatspeed, sail conservatively and work your way back through the fleet. If you have only average speed, take a gamble by sailing out to one lay line; you may pull back, but if things go wrong be prepared to discard the race.

Windshifts

All too often there is a windshift just after the start. If you're hit by a header tack as soon as you can — if the boats to windward persist on starboard it may be worth ducking them rather than getting carried on indefinitely. A lift is also a problem, because the boats to windward pull ahead. My advice is to keep going and wait for the wind to head again. Only if you're sure that the wind is going to shift more and more to the right should you tack and duck behind the fleet.

Tacking onto port

Advising people to tack onto port after a bad start is all very well, but the first problem is to find room to tack! If the other boats are more or less in line, then slow down, bear away and tack as soon as you can.

When the other boats are *not* in line, getting onto port is harder. In figure 1, boat A is prevented from tacking by B to windward and must do everything she can to make B tack. This includes pinching hard and, if necessary, suggesting to B that she's going the wrong way! When B tacks, A should wait a few moments before following suit, or she'll drop into B's lee bow on the new tack.

One very good time to tack is when another boat acts as a 'blocker' to leeward. If A and B tack at the moment shown in figure 1, C will protect them from the rest of the fleet approaching on starboard. A and B can then concentrate on sailing fast on port, secure in the knowledge that starboard boats would have to sail 'through' C to hit them.

The killer to watch out for is a boat tacking on top of you as you go about (figure 2). You then have no

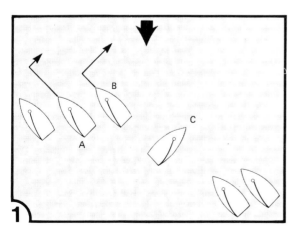

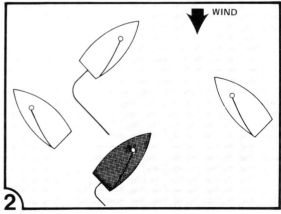

Above: Crossing behind the fleet on port tack is made less disastrous by the lift from the starboard tackers' sails.

escape, since you're covered whether you stay on port or tack back onto starboard. In some classes you get warning that the boat ahead is going to tack – in a Dutchman the familiar flip of the jibsheet, or in a Soling the crewmen beginning to raise themselves from the fully hiked position. But in other classes you get no warning, so keep your eyes open – and be particularly careful of headers, since that's the usual reason for the boats ahead tacking.

Tacking back into a hole

Most books recommend crossing behind the other boats until a hole opens up, then tacking back onto starboard into the hole. My experience is that this advice should be treated with great caution, because the tack usually puts you back where you started – with boats slightly ahead of you on each side. Then the whole depressing business begins again!

The sort of hole that you *can* take advantage of is shown in figure 3. It's fairly large, and the boat on the far side (D) is doing rather badly. Provided black can scoot close behind E and make a good tack just to leeward of D, the manoeuvre may come off. And if D experiences a header while all this is going on, so much the better!

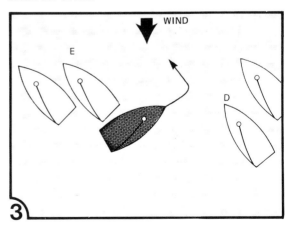

WIND

Recovering from a bad gate start

For a few moments after a gate start most of the boats are in line — there are usually few stragglers at this stage. If your start is poor, tack onto port immediately and sail behind the whole fleet to the right-hand side of the course. You'll find as you go across that the starboard boats deflect the wind, so you're sailing on a permanent lift which compensates for the blanketing of the boats ahead. If the fleet really is in line you will only lose a length or two carrying out this manoeuvre — and if the right-hand side is fastest you could find yourself ahead at the weather mark.

The only problem is if there are some stragglers.

Cross them if you possibly can, and if in doubt shout "do you want me to tack?" Nine times out of ten they'll wave you on, because the last thing they want is for you to tack on their lee bow. If they do insist on their rights bear away behind them, as there is little to be gained by tacking at this stage.

Having accepted that you messed up the start, put it out of your mind. Once you have decided what action to take to rectify the fault, settle down, relax and sail as fast as you can. "Not all races are won by the boat with the best start" — you now have the opportunity to prove the truth of that saying!

9 Shifts on the beat

The best way of checking shifts is, of course, to use your compass. But it's a mistake to watch it *all* the time; that way you miss waves and may not miss other boats. The best technique is to concentrate on sailing fast while glancing at the compass every 30 seconds or so. If you think there's been a shift, check the compass. Most of the time you will have imagined the shift and should sail on — in other words use the compass to give you the confidence *not* to tack. Press on with all speed for another 30 seconds and check your bearing again. Remember: on starboard, if the figures grow smaller it's a header. On port, if the figures grow larger it's a header.

Sometimes you need not bother with the numbers. If there is a prominent feature on the compass dial

(such as *East*) near the lubber line you can use their relative positions to give you a good feel for the shifts. For this reason compasses with coloured sectors are particularly easy to use. You can, of course, spot shifts in other ways — fortunately for boardsailors (who are not allowed compasses)! The simplest method is to watch the boat to leeward. In a header both of you bear away and the boat to leeward appears to pull ahead — this is the time to tack. The opposite happens in a lift.

Sometimes you find yourself steering towards a buoy or a prominent feature on shore. This gives a

Opposite: watching boats to leeward of you on the beat will indicate if you are being headed or lifted.

good opportunity for checking your course and spotting shifts; but in general you should be concentrating on the boat, not the shore.

Using the boats ahead

If you're behind a group of boats you can use them as a shift indicator. If they're headed, for example, watch carefully to see if the header lasts. If it does, then when the shift reaches your sails you will have the confidence to tack immediately.

Is it a real shift?

If you don't have anyone ahead you will have to judge if an apparent shift is just a hiccup in the wind, or is going to last long enough to be useful. Under these circumstances I like to wait five to ten seconds when a header strikes — if it lasts that long, then I tack.

Assuming the wind direction stays constant, a gust will initially seem like a lift because of its effect on the apparent wind. In figure 1 the wind gusts and, because the boat has not had time to speed up, the apparent wind swings 6° aft. By contrast your sails flap when you sail into a lull, which may suggest a header. Both effects are cancelled out when the boat has speeded up (to match the gust) or slowed down (in the lull). In an adverse current another factor comes into play — the tide wind. This accentuates the heading effect as the wind drops.

So in gusts and lulls, and particularly in current, be careful. Make sure that the wind really has shifted before you tack! If you're not sure it has shifted, sail on until you are positive what to do.

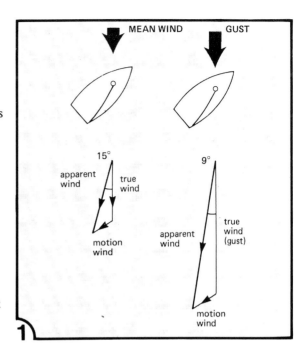

MEAN WIND   GUST

15°
apparent wind   true wind
motion wind

9°
true wind (gust)
apparent wind
motion wind

1

How often to tack?

Each boat has a minimum tacking frequency. In a Dutchman, for example, if we find ourselves tacking more than once every two minutes then we ignore the shifts, because it takes nearly that long to tack and build up speed. In a singlehander you may be able to tack on 30-second shifts, whereas in a catamaran you'd try to avoid tacking at all!

The key point here is to know how long it takes your particular boat to build up to her full speed after

a tack, and not to attempt another until you have achieved that speed.

Sometimes you get out of phase with the shifts — each time you tack the wind shifts back and you get thoroughly confused. If this happens stay on one tack, watching your compass until you're in synch — then start throwing tacks again.

Boat-to-boat in windshifts

Often you can't tack on windshifts because of another boat to weather. In this position you must do every-thing possible to make the other boat tack so that you can follow suit. You could try luffing, shouting "header — let's tack" or calling for water on a star-board-tack boat — anything to get off the bad shift and get going the right way.

Sometimes you can see a big shift coming because the boats on one side of the course are lifted contin-uously. Even if you're on a small lift it will pay to tack across towards the new wind. This often happens when there's a black cloud hovering out to that side — so in these conditions watch the clouds and your competitors extra carefully.

10 Meeting other boats on the beat

The other boats are obstacles you have to avoid on the beat. Your objective is to dispense with them as quickly as possible and get on with sailing your own race.

Two equally placed boats

The classic port vs starboard incident is where the boats are on a collision course and are level. The first point to note is that the initiative lies with the port tack boat. She must keep clear of the starboard tacker, but can choose how she does it — either by bearing away behind her rival or by tacking. The starboard tack boat has no alternative when they are fairly close but to sail straight ahead since any manoeuvring on her part counts as misleading her opponent. In figure 1, black should bear off behind white easing sheets to pick up speed and making use of the lift from white's sails. Black will lose very little and keeps her flexibility since she can now continue on port or tack later. If the starboard side of the course is favoured black will come out ahead of white.

Port tack boat slightly ahead

Even if the port tack boat is slightly ahead of the star-board tack boat she will lose less by bearing away than by tacking. With a somewhat larger lead the port tacker has the option of tacking and trying to put a lee-bow on the other boat. This may be worth doing if

(a) the left side of the course is favoured
(b) the starboard tack boat is laying the mark

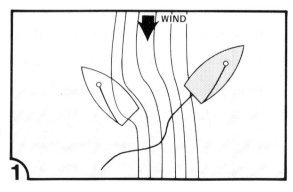

1

E-35 bears off behind the starboard tacker rather than lose ground by tacking.

(c) there are more starboard tackers behind her — the port tacker would then have to bear away several boat-lengths to pass behind them all

(d) the port tacker made a poor start and is tacking into a hole in the line of starboard boats.

The objective of the lee-bow is to deflect wind onto the wrong side of the other boat's sails (see figure 2).

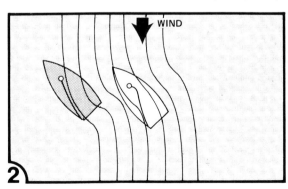

WIND

2

To be effective black must be almost level with white and close (the distance varies from class to class but is probably about one length on average). If the lee-bow is successful, white will soon drop back and be forced to tack — so both boats lose a tack. But if things go wrong white will drive over the top of black and kill her speed.

The other snag with the manoeuvre is that black loses the initiative. She's trapped to leeward of white and can't tack again until white either tacks off or drops well back. Meanwhile she may be missing wind-shifts.

Once the lee-bow is established you can put the screws on the other boat by pinching — but beware of doing this too soon after the tack or the windward boat may sail over the top of you!

If you're on starboard

There's nothing worse than having someone tack on your lee bow. It may be worth foregoing your star-board rights and waving a port tacker across your bows to avoid this situation. Consider also slowing

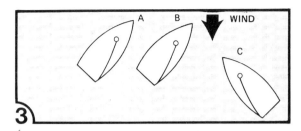

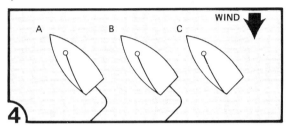

down and/or bearing away to encourage her to go across. Once she's out of the way you can get going again with no worries – and you'll be much faster alone than locked into a dogfight.

If a port tacker ignores your invitation to cross and tacks under your lee bow, tack off as soon as it's clear

you're not going over the top of her. If you wait too long her backwind will slow you down and your concentration will go. She can't risk losing speed by two tacks in quick succession, so if you tack off quickly she will probably carry on, and you'll be rid of her.

If you're on port

A word of warning: if you're on port, a starboard tacker waves you across and a collision occurs, the other skipper's encouragement for you to carry on cannot be used in your defence.

Three boats meeting

A typical encounter is shown in figure 3. Boat B has the initiative: she can bear off behind C (giving A room to follow suit) or call for water to tack (giving A time to respond). Other things being equal, bearing away is better than tacking because tacking leaves B sandwiched between the other boats (figure 4). However, if B finishes up on the lay line, tacking may pay and she may take both A and C!

11 The windward mark

The best way to approach the windward mark is in the lead! This is the only way you can normally plan an ideal rounding: further down the fleet and you'll find yourself converging with a dozen or more rivals, all keen to get onto the reach and away. You can make – or lose – many places at the windward mark, the more so in a large fleet.

The ideal route to the mark

If there are no special wind or current considerations, the ideal route is to beat up the middle of the course

keeping in phase with the shifts. Your aim is to sail along the lay line for as short a distance as possible, thus minimising the chance of having to approach the mark on a header. You should also aim only just to clear the mark – in the absence of other boats there's nothing to be gained by overstanding it. Unfortunately, your rivals seldom let you sail the ideal route!

Why is the lay line approach poor?

Coming in to the mark on a long starboard hitch seldom pays. Firstly, the further you are from the

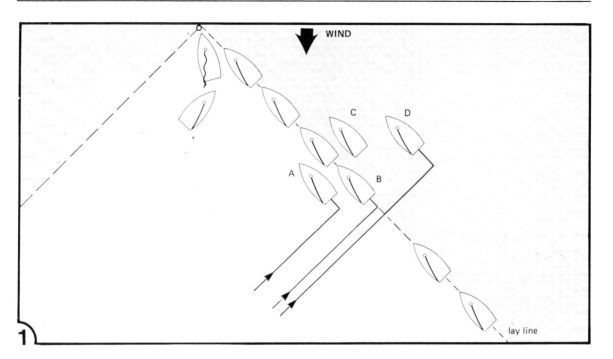

mark the harder it is to judge when you're *on* the lay line. You might well find you're overstood, with consequent loss of time (and distance). Secondly, once you're on the lay line you can't respond to windshifts. A lift will make you overstand the mark, while a header will bring up the boats to leeward. Finally, as you get near the mark boats may tack ahead or to weather of you, forcing you to either plough on in dirty air or tack yourself – over the lay line. Therefore deliberately under-stand and put in a short port hitch nearer the mark.

Rounding in a bunch

Although the middle route is great when you're ahead, there are problems in using it further down the fleet. As you come in on port you'll often be confronted with a long line of starboard tackers (see figure 1). Don't tack to leeward of the line (like A) as the chances of pinching round the mark are slim. The only time you can get away with it is on smooth water in relatively light winds with the current against you (or better still under you). In these circumstances most people will overstand, letting you come in beneath them.

Even tacking into a small hole (like boat B) leads

Right: boardsailors converging on the windward mark.

to problems. You are obliged to keep clear of the boat behind while you're tacking – which isn't easy. Even harder is picking up speed after the tack: you're sailing in disturbed air and water which make it difficult to get going. B also has the disadvantage of beginning the reach to leeward of C and D.

The best course of action is to bear away until you can see a reasonably sized hole and sail right through it, tacking when you're in clear air (D). You gain

The port-tack Laser is about to take a sighting as she passes behind her rival to see if she's on the lay line. But at the crucial moment the starboard tacker bears off, misleading 102536 into carrying on well beyond the lay line.

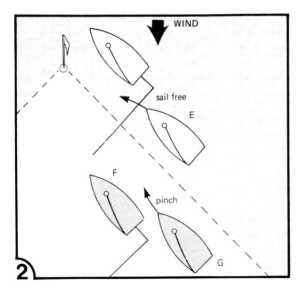

quite a bit of speed as you reach down towards the hole and, by tacking late, finish up well to windward of the bunch who tend to squeeze and slow as they struggle to keep their wind clear.

If you know you're going to round in a bunch the best policy is to come across on port so you hit the lay line about 25-75 metres from the buoy. There should be a hole there so pass through it and tack. The further down the fleet you are the more bunched the boats are likely to be, so look for that gap earlier and tack across for it. But do try to avoid joining the lay line ridiculously early.

Encouraging the port tacker

If you're sure you can lay the mark (i.e. have something in hand) you want to discourage other boats from tacking in front of you. As they cross you point 10° lower (E in figure 2); they will think you're understanding and carry on across your bows, leaving you room to squeeze inside at the mark.

If you're not laying, on the other hand, pinch as the opposition cross you to mislead them into thinking you're on course for the mark. F will, hopefully, tack early leaving G to tack off into clear air and perhaps catch her on starboard at the mark.

You can also mislead boats passing behind you in a similar way (see photos opposite).

One-sided beats

Sometimes the beat is one-sided; in this case, always sail the long leg first. You will find it much easier to judge when to tack for the windward mark when the mark is nearby. It is virtually impossible to judge your tack correctly if you're a leg away. Equally important, sailing the long tack first keeps you away from the lay line.

Simultaneous tacking

Beware the simultaneous tacker. In the situation shown in figure 3, it is X's intention to tack as soon as Y has passed astern and then carry her on until X can safely lay the mark. In this way X would be certain to round first. But if Y tacked at the same time as X, X would be disqualified because she is on Y's port side.

If Y is well known for this manoeuvre, X should continue on starboard a little further than usual before tacking. If Y stays on port X can always sail free to prevent her tacking for the mark — and if Y tries a simultaneous tack X has room to bear off behind her.

Don't hit the mark!

Leave enough room between yourself and the buoy to let out your boom — especially in strong winds. In some classes you also need room to lift your centreboard before rounding. And give the buoy a wide berth when you're beating against the tide — twice the distance you thought you'd need. The objective is to round in a professional way, not scrape round with your heart pounding!

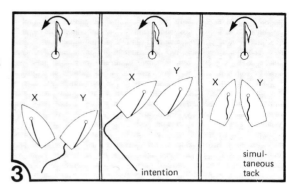

intention

simul-
taneous
tack

ROUNDING TO STARBOARD

Olympic courses are normally set so the marks are left to port. However, we are sometimes sent round the other way; the most important differences occur at the windward mark, and it's these that I want to concentrate on here.

Two boats on the lay line

If two boats approach nose-to-tail on the lay line as in the photo sequence below, then the leader has problems rounding the mark. She may not tack ahead of the following boat, which can carry her past the mark and tack round first. If the leader is clever she can avoid this in one of two ways. She could slow down once she's within two boat-lengths of the mark; this would force the boat behind to dive outside, leaving the first boat free to pick up speed and tack round first. Alternatively, she could luff head to wind as she reaches the mark like 102536 in the photo sequence. Note that this is not tacking since a tack only begins when the boat passes *beyond* head to wind. Once again, 91147 can only round outside, so 102536 leaves the mark first.

Leaving the windward mark to starboard. The leading boat luffs head to wind to avoid being carried past the mark (see above).

Boats on opposite tacks

A useful tactical manoeuvre for an approaching port-tack boat is shown in the photo sequence opposite. Although 102536 has right of way over 91147, she cannot tack ahead of her. By careful manipulation of her speed, 91147 can force 102536 to cross in front of her, then scoot round the starboard tacker's stern and luff around the mark first. The secrets are for 91147 to adjust her speed in good time so she can pass behind her rival, to shout to 102536 not to tack and then to reach behind her getting up enough speed to luff around the mark.

If 102536 reckons she's going to have this trick played on her, the solution is to slow down and (if necessary) luff head to wind around the mark, preventing 91147 getting behind. Once 91147 is committed to going to windward of 102536 then the usual shout of "starboard" will put her about and 102536 can then tack round the mark at leisure.

Rounding in a bunch

It often happens that a large group of boats arrives at the mark on starboard. If you're in the centre of the course, keep an eye open and if there are holes in the group sail through them on port, tack and approach on starboard. If the group is solid it may be worth trying a port-tack approach. Overstand the mark by several lengths and keep a close watch on the starboard boats since they may carry on beyond the mark just to hit you. However, if they do tack round properly you'll come away from the mark well placed – going fast and to windward of the bunch.

Above: a useful trick for a port-tack boat at the windward mark (see text). Below left: after the rounding 100302 just manages to slip through in front of the approaching starboard tackers.

Rounding onto the run

A bunch of starboard tackers can be a menace if the next leg is a run. They stop you bearing away and you are often forced to go right round them (course Y in figure 4) before you can get onto the run. There's also the opportunity for unscrupulous rivals to luff, opening up a tempting hole, and then sail free to hit you.

If at all possible, slip through a gap (100302 in the photo below): not only do you zoom off downwind right away, but you're immediately on the right side of the course to get an overlap at the leeward mark.

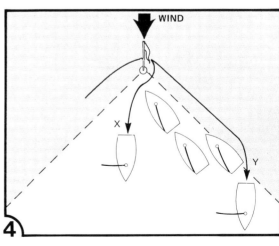

12 Learning from the first beat

As you approach the first mark it's worth taking a moment to analyse which (if any) was the fast route up the beat. On an Olympic course you will have to sail the beat at least three more times, so you really need this information.

Firstly, think about your own boatspeed. Were you going faster or slower than the boats around you? This will give an indication if your own route up the beat was a good one — for instance, if you reckon you were pretty fast relative to your neighbours but arrived at the mark in a poor position, then your route was suspect. Next, look where the boats who went left and right finished up. If there's a gradation across the course — e.g. the right-hand boats did well, the left-hand boats badly and the middle-course boats came out in the middle — then this implies a wind bend or a tidal difference across the course. Often the effect will be caused by wind deflection over the shore (see chapter 2). If you reckon there is a gradation, you should definitely consider going towards the fast side next time round.

Often the picture is confused, with boats from the left and the right side coming out ahead of you. This implies that getting the shifts right was the most important factor — so next time concentrate more on the shifts. This may mean going up the middle of the course, though sometimes you will be forced towards one side by the shifts themselves.

If one side seems faster, is the effect static or will that side become more and more favoured during the

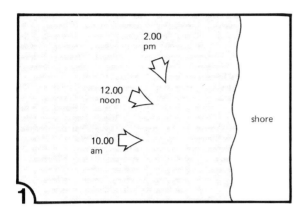

1

day? For instance, a strengthening breeze can often cause the wind to swing gradually 'with the sun' as in figure 1, in which case it will pay to hold port tack for some time after rounding the leeward mark — even though you are sailing into a header.

As you round the weather mark, remember to look for current flowing past it. Waves tend to confuse the picture so look more than once and also try to spot the lay of the buoy's mooring line. Then feed this current information into your first beat analysis.

Test your theory

Even if all the indications are that (say) the left side of the course pays, I'd be very unwilling to go out on a limb to the extreme left-hand side. I'd rather test my theory on the second lap in the following way.

Shortly after the leeward mark head towards the side that has taken your fancy and pick a boat that is going the other way. Then watch to see how you're faring relative to your 'marker'. If you're gaining then keep going to your chosen side; if not, tack back before it's too late. This check is usually pretty accurate; the speed of the 'marker' is likely to be very similar to your own since you have just ended the first lap close together.

Sometimes the course is so biased that there is only one way to go. One of the most difficult regattas to win was the Flying Dutchman World Championship in Adelaide. The adverse current was much weaker inshore and the wind was amazingly steady so the only thing to do was blast out to the port lay line and tack for the weather mark. It's easy to lose concentration in a race like that, because you don't have to think much. The only place to be in such a procession is in the lead!

Tides, currents and drift

I prefer to talk about a flow of water because the movement can be caused by many things: the *tide*, a *current* (perhaps caused by barometric pressure changes, as you get in the Baltic) or *drift* — where the surface of the water in warm climates is blown along

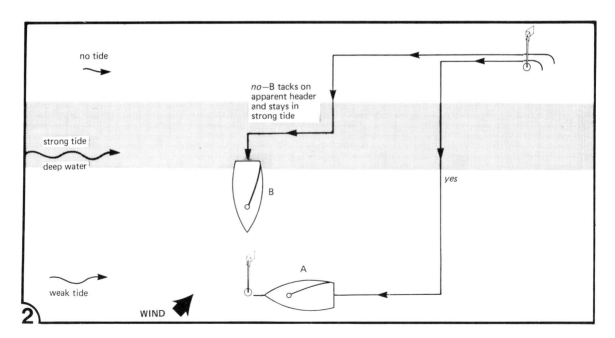

2

by the wind. In the Mediterranean, for example, there is often little wind and no drift in the morning, but a good breeze and a 2-knot current (straight downwind) in the afternoon.

Tides are predictable, and you can learn a lot about them by looking at a large-scale chart before a regatta. Before you go afloat check the time of high water and work out the expected direction of flow during the race. If you are an experienced sea sailor you should be able to tell if the tide has turned from the different wave patterns that form. If you can't do this, check the water flowing past each mark as you round it. Watch too for tide lines — these streaks on the water indicate that the tide is flowing in opposite directions on each side of the line. In this case a small deviation in course across the line can gain (or lose!) you a good distance.

Currents are harder to identify. In the pre-Olympic regatta in Tallinn there was a header halfway up the beat on starboard. Many crews were tacking on this, although boats that sailed on through the header

Flying Dutchmen approaching the windward mark. This is the time to analyse your performance on the beat.

seemed to do better and were eventually lifted again. We had checked the current at the start and found there was none — so the whole thing seemed a mystery. Eventually we spotted a fishing mark which showed a current flowing across the middle of the course (figure 2). The chart showed deeper water in this area, which confirmed our suspicion that the boats which tacked on the 'header' had simply gone straight into a foul current, whereas those that ploughed on came into the mark on port in slacker water.

The reach

The shifts and water flow also have implications for the reaching legs. If, for instance, there is a permanent shift then one will be closer than the other. Checking the current at the windward mark will tell you whether to aim off on the reach to allow for it.

Nothing is worse than having an understanding of the course dawn on you just as you reach the finish. You need that understanding at the end of the first round. Keep your eyes open, talk to your crew, formulate and test your theory — then go the fast way.

13 The reach

The end of the beat is the first time you're sure of your position. Now you can settle down and put some distance between yourself and your pursuers or, more likely, set about catching up the leaders.

As you approach the windward mark, try to spot the gybe mark. If you can't see it you'll need to sail on a bearing (see chapter 3) until the buoy comes into sight. If you can see the next mark, take a transit on it as soon as you get on the reach. If you want to sail the rhumb line (the shortest course to the mark) all you have to do is keep checking your transit.

The ideal course

The shortest distance between two points is a straight line, so this is your ideal course. In winds less than force 4 you should deviate slightly, luffing up in lulls and bearing away in gusts. In this way you meet the gusts earlier and stay with them longer. But remember to keep checking your transit, since your average course should be the rhumb line. In force 4 and above keep a straighter course, since the gusts reach you very quickly. This ideal course is slightly modified if you're flying a spinnaker (which I'll deal with on page 44).

Tide

If the tide is setting across the reach, your transit becomes even more useful. You'll find you need to 'aim off' in order to keep travelling the shortest distance. Figure 1 shows the classic case where the tide is pushing boats up to windward. Most helms luff on the reach anyway, and the tide adds to this effect. The result is that most of the fleet sails a great arc (like A) and finishes up running into the mark, leaving B to make huge gains.

I have used this tactic on many occasions but the one that sticks in my mind was the Olympic trials in Poole Bay. Although I reached the weather mark only eighth, most of those ahead luffed hard after rounding. By sailing on the rhumb line I had passed most of them by gybe mark and had an overlap on the rest. Once in the lead we were able to hold our position and, as it turned out, win selection.

If the tide is setting to leeward, you must luff above the rhumb line initially. This helps keep your wind clear from the boats around, and allows for the wind dropping later in the leg. To go below the rhumb line is usually disastrous – if you miscalculate you may not even be able to lay the mark, and will finish up beating to it.

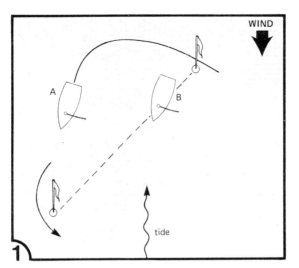

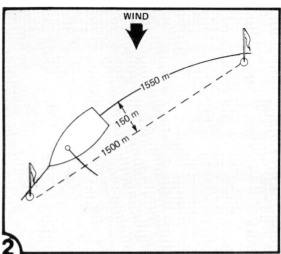

Flying a spinnaker will affect the course you sail on a reach (see page 44).

Up or down on the reach?

In a large fleet most boats luff on the reach, trying to keep their wind clear and a huge 'bow' develops. The question is, should you sail the 'great circle' or risk going down to leeward? The most important point to remember is, only luff if you're threatened. If no one is likely to take your wind, sail straight for the next mark! If you are threatened, nine times out of ten you have to luff. Sooner or later the boats behind you are going to have to bear off for the mark, so you may not have to go too far. Provided you luff gradually, you won't lose too much; for example in figure 2 you only lose 50 m by sailing the windward course, although you went 150 m off the rhumb line.

Now, what about the one chance out of ten, when sailing to leeward of the rhumb line can pay off?

(a) If the tide is setting to windward on the reach, a leeward course can be dramatically effective.

(b) If there is a large group ahead and a gap behind, go to leeward if the group begins to luff.

(c) If there's a large group behind which begins to luff, keep on the rhumb line until they begin to threaten your wind. Then either luff or bear away in time to prevent them blanketing you.

(d) If you're at the back of the fleet you might as well try a leeward course — you have nothing to lose and will, in any case, keep clear of the cowboys around you.

(e) On a broad reach it may well pay to go to leeward. The windshadows of the boats ahead are angled forwards, which keeps them clear of your

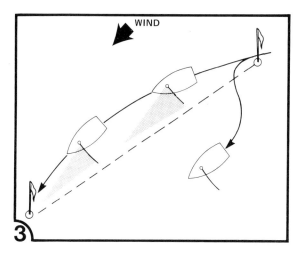

sails (figure 3). The boats luffing will have a slow run in to the mark – and in a big group people tend to luff more than usual because the gain in speed is more spectacular.

If you decide to go to leeward, try to bear off in a gust or on a wave; in this way you may actually gain while you go down. And never bear off onto a dead run – the objective is to slide down not stop! You will, of course, need to finish up well to leeward of the other boats to be confident your wind is clear.

Once down to leeward, stay down. Hold on so you come in to the mark on a beam reach; you need to be on the fastest point of sailing here to get through windshadows and claim the largest number of overlaps. It often feels as if you're holding on too long – but *keep low* (figure 4) or you risk losing everything by coming up too early right in the lee of the boats running down to the mark.

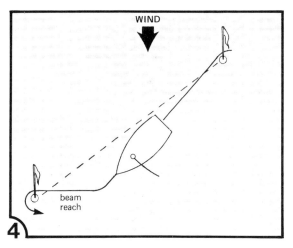

The effect of a spinnaker

In strong winds you have to bear off in gusts to prevent the spinnaker overpowering you – so you will have to go to weather of the rhumb line in the lulls. If the reach is close and you're dubious about carrying the spinnaker, luff slightly as you round the windward mark with a view to hoisting later. Your objective is to luff far enough so you can carry the spinnaker right to the gybe mark. Boats to leeward will lose out if they are forced to lower the spinnaker to lay the mark, only to hoist it again after the gybe.

Another reason for not going down to leeward on a close spinnaker reach is that you don't gain speed by luffing at the gybe mark.

As always, though, there are exceptions – for example, keep down if there is an enormous raft of boats ahead of you, all luffing to the horizon!

Luffing another boat

In most circumstances you will need to luff on the reach. Your aims in this are to hold your position, to keep your wind clear, but to deviate from the rhumb line as little as possible.

Firstly, size up the boat behind you. If the skipper is the type who enjoys luffing 'all the way' it may pay you to let him go, particularly if he's faster than you

and there aren't any other boats right behind him. As he begins to go for your weather, act boldly (a small luff here won't cost you much). Make sure you or your crew watch him all the time. If he thinks no one is looking, he's bound to go to weather. But a bold luff and an icy stare may persuade him to go to leeward.

This tactic paid off handsomely for me in a major ton event in Helsinki. The boat I was sailing, Manzanita, was being pursued by a light displacement centreboarder, which was far faster on the reach in medium winds. My initial bold luffs forced her to leeward; her helmsman didn't bear off enough and we were able to keep her in our windshadow for the whole of that leg and then cover her upwind to the finish.

If your pursuer continues to luff, you've got to respond. After each luff, reconsider your position. Is it costing you relative to other boats? If not, carry on luffing. If it is, consider not responding. But remember, by the halfway point he's going to have to bear away to get back down to the mark, so your problems lessen as the reach goes on.

It may help to establish yourself a reputation as a crazy luffer. Use a practice race to take someone miles out to windward — and make sure everyone is looking. Next time, they'll think twice before going to windward of you!

The group of Lasers on the right are starting to luff. 100302 is just clear of their windshadows; she can either follow suit to keep her wind clear or bear away to gain distance on the luffers.

Being luffed by a boat ahead

Before going to weather of someone, think carefully. Is it worth while? Are you faster? It's no good going out of your way to overtake a faster boat since she'll come past you again later. What about other boats? If you may lose one other boat it's worth the risk, but the possibility of losing two others is unacceptable.

If you decide to luff, do it when no one on the other boat is looking. And try to luff smoothly — jerky alterations of course lose ground.

Ian Macdonald-Smith and I worked out a successful spinnaker luffing routine which helped us win the Flying Dutchman Championships in Naples. We would respond, luff for luff, to the other boat. Then when the helmsman looked away, we would drop the kite. When he looked back it was all over, since there's no way a boat with a spinnaker can luff one without — so we got through to weather. For some reason, the other skipper never thinks of dropping his own spinnaker and carrying on the fight!

14 The gybe mark

The gybe mark is all too often rounded in a heaving tangle of sheets, spinnaker and crew's limbs. Yet you can gain a good number of places by a cool, clean rounding. You should have two main aims as you come in to the mark.

1 You need to obtain the inside track — if you have to round the mark outside other boats you will not only have further to sail, but also increase your chances of being run into from either side. If you turn next to the mark then, in theory at least, you can only get clobbered by boats outside you. Most important of all, the boat making the inside turn will start the next reach as far to windward as possible, avoiding her rivals' windshadows.

2 You must give yourself enough room to make a good rounding. Start making your turn at least a length away from the mark, so that you can (almost) clip it as you *finish* the rounding (figure 1). In a tight bunch you will often be forced close to the mark on your approach, which means you swing wide during your turn; it's up to you to call to the boats outside for plenty of water so you have the space you need to carve a graceful turn.

Overlap rules at the gybe mark

If you want to turn inside another boat, you must be overlapping her when her bow enters a two-length circle around the mark. Everything is judged at the moment when the leading boat's bow hits that circle. In figure 2, if B's bow is past the dotted line (drawn abeam through A's aftermost point) then B can round inside A. If B is further back than this, she will have to round outside (or behind) A. Note that the dotted line is drawn through A's aftermost point: in a dinghy this will be her rudder, *not* her transom.

Note also that, provided B has an overlap at the two-length circle, she can turn inside even if A subsequently breaks the overlap by accelerating, turning or otherwise. Similarly, if B has *not* established an overlap at two lengths, she will not gain any rights if she manages later to shoot inside A.

Opposite: the gybe mark is often the scene of much confusion. In this Flying Dutchman fleet, LX-10 has lost her spinnaker; L-7 has made a good rounding but has pointed too high too soon (the crew is not yet on the wire).

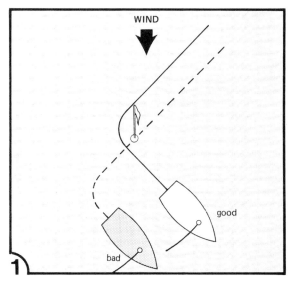

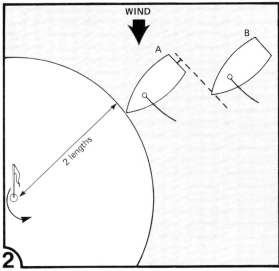

A two-boat duel

When two boats are in contention at the end of the
first reach the leading boat often luffs. Figure 3 shows
the inevitable result — the pursuing boat (D) is able to
blanket the leader on the run down to the mark. And
the further C luffs the more time she gives D to
blanket her.

If you do find yourself well out to windward with
another boat on your heels, slow down and let her
sail over you. She's now on the wrong side as you
approach the mark; you have the overlap and the
inside turn.

Naturally, if you're behind another boat try the
opposite tactic. First try to get your overlap to leeward. If this fails, encourage the other boat to luff
you. Avoid going through her wind, and blanket her
as she bears off for the mark. At the last minute
swerve aside to gain an overlap and the inside turn.

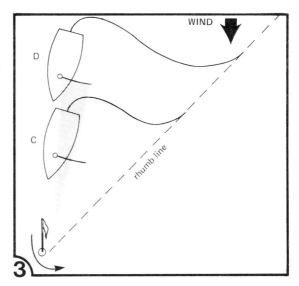

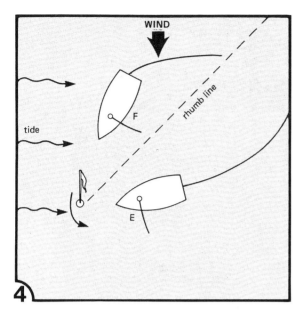

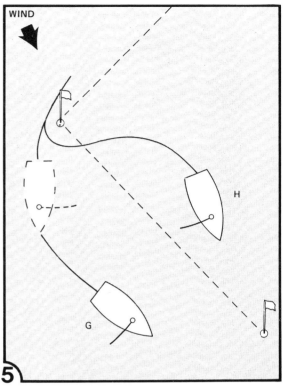

Tide

If the tide is against you or pushing you to windward, try to approach the mark from a leeward course (like E in figure 4). Having to broad reach in to the mark is really slow, and will lose F many places.

After the gybe mark

If the wind backs permanently the first reach will be very close and the second reach almost a run; you may even need to tack downwind in light airs. In these circumstances most of the fleet will gybe round the mark and luff (like H in figure 5) so it may pay to delay your gybe and continue on starboard for a while to keep your wind clear (like G).

15 The run

Running is slow. So although there is only one run in a race, it takes up a disproportionate amount of time. It follows that good running technique can gain you a lot of places — especially if you're behind and can blanket the boats ahead.

The most important aspect of the run is keeping your wind clear. This takes priority over all other tactics.

Tacking downwind

The next consideration is tacking downwind. Most singlehanders go fast downwind because their masts are not supported by stays and they can get their booms out square. This is not the case with boats that have shrouds, which means that it pays in most classes to broad reach one way, gybe and broad reach back.

Tacking downwind is effective because it increases the apparent wind. In figure 1 one boat is running at 4 knots dead before a 10-knot breeze. Her apparent wind is only 6 knots (because her sails are moving away from the real wind, reducing its effect). The other boat has decided to tack downwind; not only has her apparent wind increased to 7.2 knots but it is blowing at a more favourable angle.

The further you deviate from the rhumb line the greater the apparent wind; the problem is that you finish up sailing a greater distance. You can only determine by experience how far to deviate from the direct course — but the faster the boat the more it pays to deviate.

Eventually you will have to decide when to gybe back to the mark and it's here that the sight lines on your deck come into their own. In a Soling and Dutchman I use the 80° line in very light winds and 30° line in strong winds; experience will tell you which angles suit your class best.

Gybing on shifts

Just as you tack on shifts on the beat, you should gybe on shifts on the run. Look at the gains made in figure 2 by A over B. Both boats sail at the fastest angle to the wind but A takes the correct gybes to keep her closer to the rhumb line.

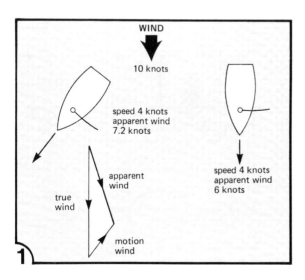

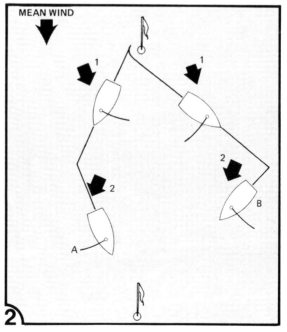

If you approach the weather mark on a header, stay on starboard after the mark (if you come in on a lift, gybe round the mark). Get onto the fastest downwind course as soon as you can (figure 3) and note the compass bearing. If the wind heads further you'll automatically bear away to keep up speed – this will show up both from the compass and from the leeward mark coming into line ahead of your bows.

A lift is harder to spot. You will automatically luff to keep up speed, and should note the change in compass bearing. In a lift consider gybing. Your gybing should be of such a standard that you lose nothing (or even gain) on each gybe. If not – practice is needed! In shifty winds running is like beating: avoid going too far to one side of the course especially near the mark – you don't want to have to run in to the buoy on the wrong shift. In fact at the mid-point of the run start looking for a shift to take you across to the inside of the turn at the leeward mark.

Planning ahead

Start thinking about the run early – certainly well before you reach the windward mark. Has the wind shifted during the beat? If so, the run will have turned

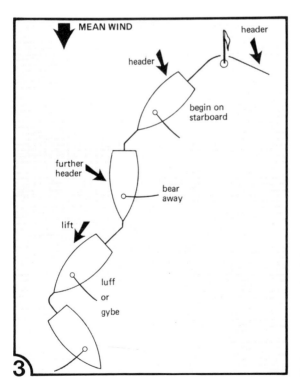

into a broad reach and you'll need to modify your tactics (see below). If the wind is shifting back and forth about its mean direction, determine if you're on a header or lift as you approach the mark and then stay on starboard or gybe onto port accordingly.

As you round the buoy check the tide – if it will be setting across the run then begin on the gybe that takes you up-tide. Also, glance astern to see if you'll be followed round by a group of boats as this will affect your plans for the run.

Very broad reach

On a very broad reach you won't have to tack downwind. If your wind is clear head straight for the leeward mark, using a transit if possible. Luff in the lulls and bear away in the gusts; in this way you meet the puffs sooner and stay with them longer. In the gusts bear off to dead downwind – or further if you can ride the waves better.

If there is a boat close on your transom, make a bold luff early to give her the message. Keep looking astern so her crew feels you mean business, but consider letting her go if luffing her will lose you several other boats.

If you round with a group right behind, you'll have to go high initially because their windshadows extend down to leeward of the rhumb line. Try to keep *just* clear of their windshadows. As you pull clear, wait for a gust to bear off back to the rhumb line – you must avoid running dead downwind on your approach to the leeward mark.

Running in light winds

In light winds look astern frequently and try to spot gusts moving towards you over the water. Then head across towards the side the gust will pass. Some experts even sail downwind standing up and facing backwards to help them spot the puffs.

Beware, however, of yawing from side to side too enthusiastically. Apart from the extra distance you have to sail, some puffs come out of a stationary cloud (or are caused by obstructions onshore) so never arrive! The other problem (which I've experienced in Rio and even the Med) is a thin patch of oil on the water, which can completely mislead you into thinking one side is calmer.

Opposite: if you approached the windward mark on a lift, gybe onto port tack after the rounding.

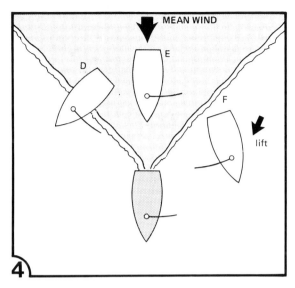

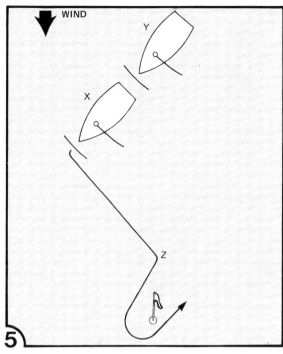

Attacking one boat ahead of you

Your attacking weapon on the run is your wind-shadow, which you can cast onto an opponent's sails from a range of up to about four mast lengths. She can defend by luffing or bearing away to keep her wind clear. Her quarter-wave also pushes you back.

One technique for overtaking a boat ahead is to ride her quarter-wave until a gust arrives. If her crew is not looking, use it to luff and power over the quarter-wave (D in figure 4). Another is to sail directly behind (like E), taking her wind to the maximum. If she luffs slowly, go to windward. If she luffs sharply dive to leeward at the last minute — especially if that will give you an overlap later. A third method is to wait for a lift and quickly gybe across her stern (F).

Approaching the leeward mark

Often you find yourself in the position of boat X in figure 5, i.e. rapidly approaching the point where you should gybe for the mark but being pursued by another boat.

In this case it is essential that you gybe first, even if the following boat gybes too early. You can always put in another gybe (at point Z); the main thing is that you've prevented Y from getting an overlap. Ignore the fact that Y will take your wind briefly as you gybe.

You must also avoid sailing on a dead run to the leeward mark; this is not only slow but will certainly allow the pursuing boat to blanket and overtake you. Once again, the sight lines on your deck will indicate when the moment to gybe is approaching.

Left: keeping your wind clear is the first priority on the run.

1

3

2

There are several options if you are attacking one rival on the run. Usually I sail right up behind her (1) taking her wind as much as I can. Then if a gust arrives I use it to power over her quarter-wave (2); if she luffs violently I bear away through her lee (3). But if a header arrives I gybe across her stern (4).

4

16 The leeward mark

Your objectives at the leeward mark and the rules that apply there are similar to those at the gybe mark (see chapter 15).

Often a whole line of boats converges on the mark (figure 1). Boat A will make the best rounding, provided she calls early for water so that the others have

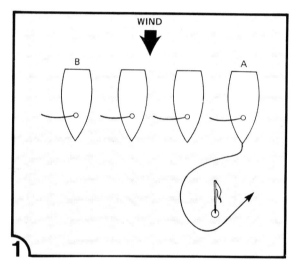

time to move out and give her room to turn properly. B will come off worst, since she will be on the outside of the turn. If you anticipate finding yourself in this position, slow down *early* by pulling the main in, steering hard or collapsing the spinnaker. Your aim is to cross behind A, establish an overlap on her and round inside the whole group. Even if you fail to do this, you will be no worse off than before.

If you're worried about a following boat getting an overlap on you at the last moment, arrange your approach so that your 'overlap line' is angled forwards. In figure 2 C's helmsman has steered a low course initially and then hardened up a little for the run in to the mark, giving D no chance of an overlap.

If you are chasing one other boat blanket her late so you shoot alongside a few lengths from the mark; this gives her little time to regain the upper hand. If you're worried about her angling her overlap line forwards (as described above), stay very close — the

Below: Laser 102536 allows 91147 to crowd her and turns too tightly around the leeward mark. 91147 is able to peel off early, round properly and luff into clear air after the mark.

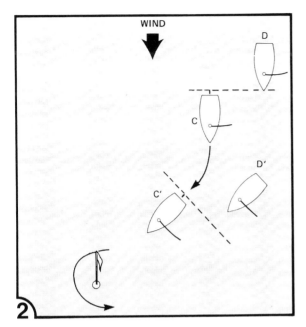

A correct rounding of the leeward mark — coming in wide and leaving it close.

effect is magnified by increased distance between the boats.

Careful jockeying from behind can sometimes force an opponent to round too close to the mark. By taking a wider sweep yourself you can build up greater speed (by using less rudder to turn), round the mark faster and luff into clear wind (see photos below).

If you don't achieve an overlap on the boat ahead, slow down and leave plenty of room between you.

Otherwise, if she makes a slow rounding you will find yourself hammering straight for her transom and having to take desperate avoiding action — since you can't hit her or the mark your only choice is to swing outside them both, which will mean you start the beat well down to leeward.

When a large number of boats arrives at the mark together, the outermost boats stack up yelling "no water!". They often stack well *outside* the two-length

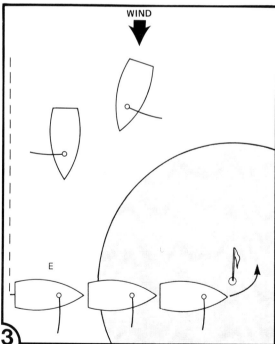

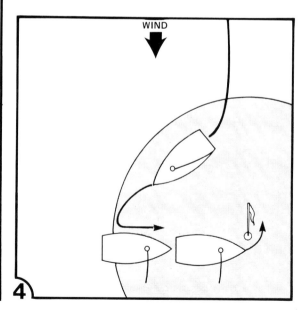

Above: 505's rounding the leeward mark. S-7351 would have done better to have slowed and rounded behind J-7000 rather than outside her.

3

4

circle, in which case you can sometimes cut inside them, despite their courteous suggestions to the contrary. In figure 3, E has stacked too wide – at this point virtually the whole fleet has an overlap on her. Rather than make E's mistake, try to get your nose inside the circle and then slow down (e.g. by pulling in your sails) and steer wide again: figure 4 shows the sort of course I have in mind.

How you come out of the mark is even more important than how you go in. If you are rounding in a line of boats you must try to avoid the lee bow of the boat ahead. You've also got to watch that the boat behind doesn't climb up to weather and stop you tacking off when the first shift comes – both will happen if you sag off after the buoy. The solution is to give a little luff as you come out of the mark: this pulls you half a length to windward of the usual track.

If the boat ahead luffs violently around the mark, however, it's pointless your luffing too. Instead try to power through her lee and luff back to close-hauled when you're in clear air.

If you have managed to avoid all the pitfalls you should come away from the mark close, fast and ready for the beat.

17 The last beat

During the first few beats it's best to avoid tacking duels with other boats. On later beats (and certainly on the final beat) you may want to protect your position by covering the boats behind. Naturally, you'll also want to avoid the cover put on you by the boats ahead. In this chapter we'll look at what cover is and how to cover one, two and more opponents.

Cover can be tight or loose (figure 1). Boat A has a tight cover on B which is firmly in her windshadow, and cannot tack off because A is so close. C, on the other hand, has a loose cover on D. Her presence doesn't slow D down, but C is in control of the situation. She's going the same way as D, so will experience the same windshifts. If D starts to threaten, C can sail a little freer to bring her windshadow to bear. Loose cover is useful if your opponent goes the same speed as you do, and if you want to avoid a tacking duel (because of a third boat nearby, for example, who might slip by while you're throwing tacks).

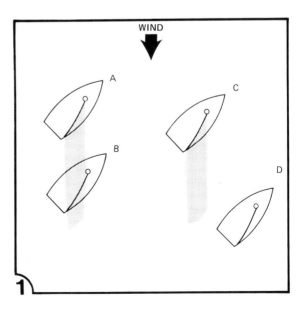

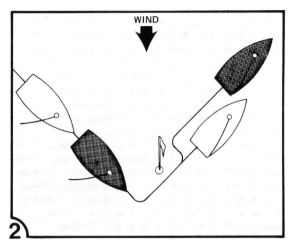

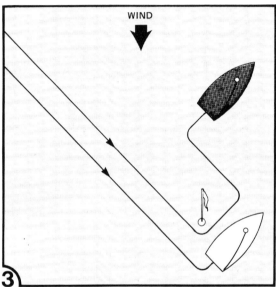

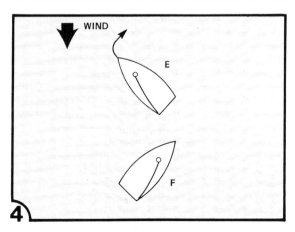

Covering one other boat

The simplest time to impose cover on another boat is at the leeward mark. If she is close behind, luff violently as you round forcing her to drop into your windshadow (figure 2). If you have a longer lead you can put in two tacks so you end up to windward of the mark as your rival rounds it (figure 3). As with all covering, you lose ground (because of the tacks) but gain a safer position. In fact, you're probably better off judging your second tack so you aren't dead to windward (i.e. get into a loose cover position) unless you want to begin a tacking duel right away.

In mid-course it's harder to establish your cover. In figure 4, E can tack on top of F. F's usual response is to tack immediately – so E must tack slowly, watching F as she does so. If F does tack, E can swing back to keep on top of her. In team racing both boats may end up head to wind; F will eventually have to bear away onto one tack and E can then follow. As usual, E will lose more than F.

The simplest method of establishing cover is deliberately to tack late so you finish up just behind the ideal covering position. Then sail for speed so you gradually take the other's wind.

Avoiding cover

In figure 2, white can either luff as she rounds the mark, or ease sheets and try to dive through black's lee as black luffs. In figure 3 white should tack as soon as she's gained speed after the mark – forcing black to tack a third time. Alternatively, white can wait until black is near one of the boats running down to the mark and tack then; black won't be able to follow suit and white breaks clear.

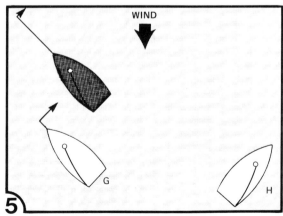

If you have nothing to lose, a series of short sharp tacks may put off the covering boat, since you'll both lose so much ground. But if you have someone really sitting on you, responding tack for tack, you'll have to resort to a dummy tack to break clear.

Warn your crew that this could be a dummy, then wait till you're sure the covering helmsman is looking. Begin to tack as usual and when the boat is head to wind, check what your opponent is doing. Now decide whether to complete the tack or fall back onto your original course, and tell your crew what you're doing.

You should be able to break clear in this way or at least slow the other boat down — in future the covering helmsman will have to tack facing backwards and the crew (who can only tack facing forwards) will soon become confused.

Stopping another boat

In the closing stages of a series you may want to slow one boat down and let another boat past — so your cover has to be really fierce. Keep close, and let your main flap. You can even pull your boom slightly to windward — which will slow you even more.

Covering two opponents

Often you will find yourself with two boats to cover. If you go for one, the other will almost certainly slip by. So how can you stay ahead of them both?

Firstly, try not to be too influenced by them. Sail to beat them both by good speed and skill. Ideally you should stay between them. Use the shifts and keep an eye on both boats. One will usually drop back — so you then 'distribute' yourself more towards the other boat. But stay between them at all times.

The most unnerving thing that can happen is when the two boats split tacks and head out to the opposite sides of the course. In this case your best bet is to put a tight cover on the nearest, forcing her to tack off and go in the same direction as the third boat (figure 5). Now loose cover her to encourage them both to keep going the same way. Re-establish your 'central' station as soon as you can — when H tacks will be the first opportunity.

Although the two of them often split tacks in the

Right: in this photo sequence I am covering two boats. One tacks off and I sit hard on the other until she tacks too. I then loose cover her across to the first, who eventually tacks back, giving me the opportunity to reposition myself midway between them.

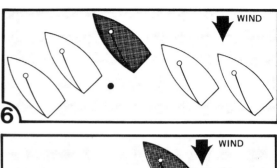

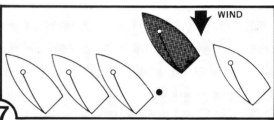

early part of the beat, after a while the second boat may become nervous and sail across to cover number three. If this happens, loose cover both of them and breathe a sigh of relief — you should certainly be able to stay ahead of them now.

Covering a group

If you find yourself trying to stay ahead of a whole bunch of boats, work out the 'centre of gravity' of the bunch (the dot in figures 6 and 7). Then tack on the shifts, staying between the 'centre of gravity' and the finish.

Above: tight cover on one boat. Below: covering a group; 91147 is well placed to stay ahead of the pack.

18 The finish

At the end of a hard race it's easy to stop concentrating – yet so often this can mean you're pipped at the post through bad tactics.

Which end of the finish line?

The finish line is seldom set at right angles to the wind. Usually one end is further to leeward, and this is the end to go for. For example, finishing at the committee boat end in figure 1 would save sailing the distance shown by the dotted line. Make your decision as you approach the finish on the lay line to one end. At the moment you cross the lay line to the other end, judge which end is nearer. In figure 2 the pin is nearer, so tack and finish right by the buoy.

Note that this method works every time, even in a strong tide because it automatically compensates for changes in apparent wind due to tide wind. For this same reason one of the most unreliable methods of assessing the finish line is to look at the flags on the committee boat – they are showing how the line lies relative to the true wind, which is irrelevant. It is important to finish *at* an end. At the start the ends are bad places to be because of the risk of getting stuck in a bunch. At the finish bunches are unlikely, so you can take the full advantage the correct end offers.

Beating one opponent to the finish

So far we've ignored the opposition. If there's just one boat behind, cover her carefully keeping between her and the nearer end of the finish line. Even if you're level you may be able to ease her out to one side by a trick known as 'shutting the barn door'. Black demonstrates this in figure 3, only tacking for the line when white is well past the committee boat. If you're caught like white, your only defence is to bear away early and tack as soon as you can *just* lay the pin. If black tries to tack to lee-bow she'll be unable to lay the pin.

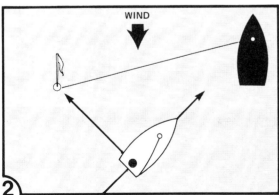

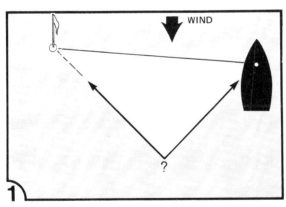

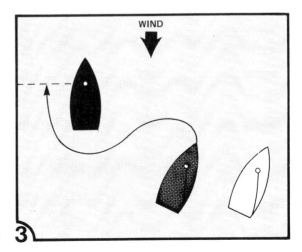

Try to finish on starboard tack if things are close.

Covering several opponents

Stay between the 'centre of gravity' of the bunch and the nearer end of the line. Black in figure 4 is perfectly placed between the dot (representing the centre of gravity of the bunch) and the port end of the line. Keep playing the shifts, but don't get out on a limb; and unless there's some special reason, don't cover one boat – your objective is to stay ahead of them all.

If you're in a bunch going for the line, try to finish on starboard tack. There's little point in getting caught port-and-starboard right in front of the OOD!

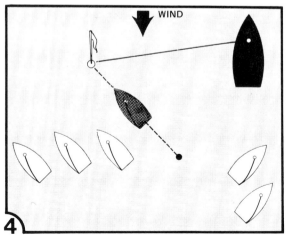

WIND

4

19 Sailing a series

The winners of major regattas usually describe their style like this: "I'm a percentage sailor" . . . "I keep to the middle of the course and work the shifts" . . . "I try not to shoot the corners" . . . "I sail the fleet".

The picture that comes across is of a careful, sensible approach, nibbling away at the opposition in each race in order to get a reasonable result rather than a brilliant win. In a championship fleet of 200 boats, for example, finishing in the first 20 in each race will give you a very good overall result, and maybe even the title. Erratic placings such as 1, 60, 120, 2, 45 . . . will get you nowhere.

Another feature of the championship winner is that he isn't greedy; his aim is to win by a few boat-lengths, not by a lap. If you are a long way ahead the chances are you took huge risks to get there; you're also well separated from the other boats which may be sailing in very different winds and current from you. Far better to 'sail the fleet' — go the same way as the bulk of the opposition, do roughly what they do but edge out slightly to the side you think is faster. Try to build a small but defensible lead. If one boat takes an extreme course you simply have to let her go; if she comes in ahead you have only lost one place, and the chances are she won't manage it again

in another race! Except in the closing stages of a series, don't duel with your favourite rivals — try to look at the fleet as a whole and keep the maximum number of boats behind you.

Perhaps most important of all, avoid protests at all costs. The hearing will be at least three hours after the incident, and it's a fact of life that witnesses will forget details and your rival may remember a different set of circumstances from those you had in mind. Often the two protestors hardly seem to have been involved in the same incident! Regrettably, there's a good chance you'll be thrown out, even if you were in the right.

So *always* avoid a collision if you can. Then the risk of being disqualified is limited, and the worry factor is reduced. But if you do hit someone, protest him and then try to forget the incident and sail normally. You'll have time to work on your case later.

Try to analyse your results objectively as the championship progresses. Did you do badly because of boatspeed, windshifts or tactics? There is no magic involved so there must be a reason for your placing. Once you find weak points in your approach you can do something about them — aim to win the last race even if the first was a disaster!

20 Racing near the shore

A proper Olympic course is always well away from land. However, many non-championship races are run near the shore for reasons of time and safety, and you need to know how to work this to your advantage.

Geographical effects

The wind usually blows in a different direction over land and water. A full discussion of this appears in David Houghton's Sail to Win book *Wind Strategy,* but a couple of good rules of thumb for beating towards the shore are:

1 If the mark is more than about half a kilometre off the shore, approaching on port tack will almost always pay.

2 If the mark is close to the shore it may be best to make the final approach on starboard tack, particularly if the air is stable.

If the windward mark is near a bay, you will often get a shift. In figure 1, for example, it pays to approach the mark on starboard, on a lift.

In the FD Worlds at Medemblik I took compass readings on the run out to the start and noticed this effect. By going right we led at the weather mark by one and a half minutes.

Beware of finding yourself in the lee of high ground. You may not only be becalmed, but vertical gusts can capsize you.

Tactics beating up the shore

If you are beating against the tide, head for the shore: the current will normally be slacker there.

On a yacht the alarm on the depth sounder should be calibrated so it goes off with a couple of inches to spare: any more than this and it will be bleeping all the time. Your best echo sounder, however, is the yacht ahead. If you keep in her line and know what she draws, you can avoid most disasters.

If you are behind another boat your only chance is to split tacks to gain clear air (and the chance of getting her on starboard when you've caught up). To break tacks will inevitably cost something: you will either need to go further out into the tide or put in two very short tacks. The short tacks are the better bet if the tide is strong.

If you are overlapped going towards the shore the situation becomes more interesting.

When the leeward boat calls for water, the windward boat must tack immediately.

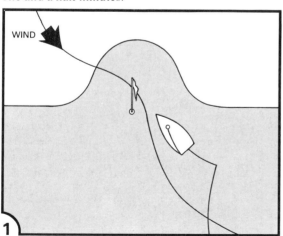

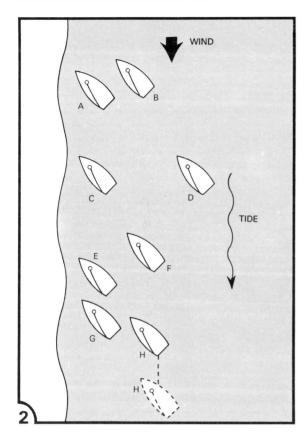

2

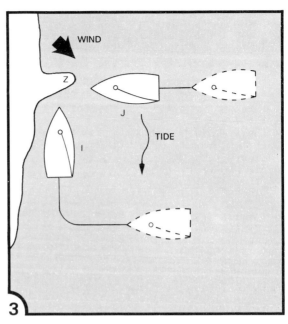

3

In figure 2 boat A can call to boat B for water to tack, giving B ample time to respond. When B tacks, A must tack immediately – she cannot sail on into slack water while B fights the tide offshore! B must tack as soon as she hears the hail: if she thinks A hailed too early, her only remedy is to protest after the tack.

When C hails D for room to tack, D can either tack or carry on, shouting "you tack". C must then tack immediately, and D must keep clear until C has completed the tack. C and D are now heading for each other and the normal port and starboard rule applies. In calling "you tack" D should have calculated that C, by tacking and then immediately bearing away, has room to clear D. If not, D herself will have to tack just after C does. By accurately judging their positions, D has a real chance to get well ahead of C here. Alternatively, D might slow a little, let C tack and cross her, and then head for the shallows with no tactical worries.

E can split tacks with F by tacking slowly and bearing away immediately, just clipping F's transom. E's helmsman should warn the crew about what is going to happen, so they don't pull the sheets in too far after the tack, allowing the boat to bear away. They should stand by to dump the main further, if necessary.

H is in a hopeless position and would do better to drop back and call "you tack" rather than be lee-bowed on the way in and covered on the way out.

In Figure 3, when you head in towards the shore on starboard, you need to think well in advance because you will be coming out on port with no rights. Boat I is too far away from J to call for water. After tacking onto port she has no rights over J, who is on starboard. She cannot call for room on obstruction Z, and has nowhere to go. She should have foreseen this earlier, and borne away immediately she tacked instead of relying on J's good nature not to T-bone her port-and-starboard.

Tactics reaching along the shore

You will often be reaching along the shore with a boat catching you from behind. Keep as close to the land as you dare. She can only poke her nose in if there is enough room to sail right through between you and the obstruction. You do not have to move out, even if she goes aground. In figure 4, M is wrong to force her way between N and the shore. However, if the overlap already exists when you reach a point two lengths from the shore, the inside boat (K) *does* have the right to sail through.

In figure 4 boat P, with no luffing rights, can sail her proper course (i.e. inshore) until boat O is unable to sail in any further. P must then keep clear, and O can call for more water if she needs to get round an obstruction.

Tactics running along the shore

All my comments on reaching also apply to running along the shore.

The problem with running is that the boats behind (Q in figure 5) blanket those ahead (R) and

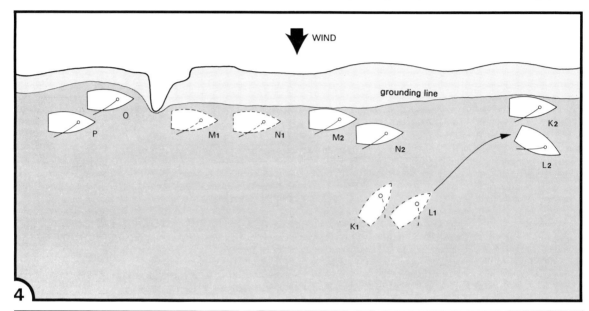

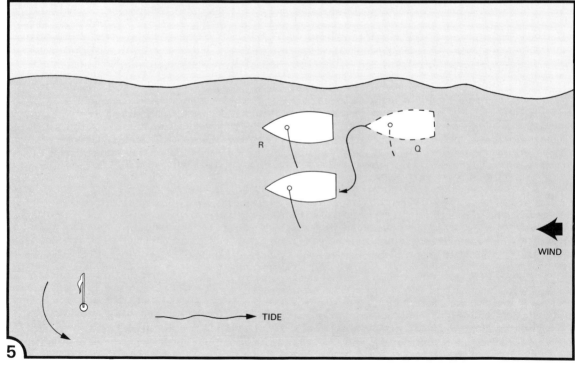

catch up rapidly. If Q can sail through between R and the shore she can go for the gap, but R has 'shut the door', forcing Q to move outside her into the tide. This slows her, and the whole process is repeated.

If you are in Q's position in a very strong tide:

1 Try your best to get inside R.

2 If the next buoy is to be left to port, attempt to blanket R at the critical moment when you both need to head offshore for the mark. Move up alongside her, gybe, and then sail out for the mark with the inside overlap.

3 If it is a long leg and you cannot get by, consider your fleet position. There may be little to be gained by slowing both of you, so think about sailing on R's lee quarter and moving in to blanket her if she looks like pulling ahead.

In a weak tide it may well pay to go further offshore, shouting to R not to sail below her proper course. With a decent gap between you, it may be possible to pull through, especially if there is a third boat close behind who will blanket R while you are zapping along in clear air.

Above & below: Downwind duelling in the annual Round the Island Race.

21 Offwind starts

No one likes offwind starts because they are unfair. This is especially so when you're starting on a beam reach or broader: the guy with the worst start can take the wind of the best starter, and hold him back for ages. Despite this many yacht races start downwind. Before looking at specifics, let's look at some general principles.

1 You've got to be on the line at the gun. If you're not, someone else will be.

2 Even more important is *clear air*. Do anything necessary to get it.

3 Use the chart to work out the distance to the first mark. If it's some way away you can afford to lose some ground to gain clear air. But if you will reach the buoy soon you can't afford to give anything away.

4 Don't go for broke at the start – you probably have three or four hours to race, so you've plenty of time to catch up. Just try to guarantee a reasonable position at the first mark.

5 *Never* set the kite until you've started unless you *know* you're going to be late. You can't manoeuvre with the spinnaker up, it's impossible to luff if you need to, and if you're over the line with the kite up it will take you forever to get back. By all means have the pole up and everything ready, but leave the sail in the bag until the gun goes.

6 With three or four minutes to go, have a good look at where the other boats are. That gives you time to avoid bunches and keep out of the way of anything bigger: both will take your wind if you're not careful.

7 You want maximum speed at the start, and must know your boat so you can get it. In light airs most boats go faster if sailed fairly high on the wind, while in strong winds most boats gain by sailing low. If a gust or lull affects you at the start, adjust your course accordingly.

8 Practising a timed run is always useful. Even if you don't do a timed run at the start, you will gain useful information. You need about 90 seconds sailing to give a reproducible result: less than this, and variations in your initial speed will throw you out. Ideally there will be a buoy the required distance from the line, but a transit is just as good (figure 1.) For the real start, aim to arrive a few seconds earlier than in practice: there will be more interference from other boats which will slow you down. In a tide, and with a fast boat such as a trimaran, a timed run is virtually the only way of being on the line at a reaching start.

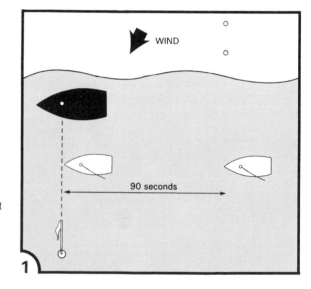

9 As with a windward start, it's also very nice to know how long it takes to sail the length of the line.

10 In a menagerie class you can often catch a tow from a faster boat, provided there is enough wind to generate a good quarter wave. But make sure it *is* a faster boat or you'll simply be trapped in the quarter wave of someone slower. On a run take the tow on her leeward quarter so you don't take her wind. There's no point in destroying her performance: you're both on the same side for once. The more the leg becomes a reach, the higher you want to go to

weather. Towing is most effective on a fast reach, with you on her weather quarterwave and quite close to her transom.

Having covered a few general principles, let's look at how to modify your starting technique as the wind gradually draws aft of the start line.

Starting to windward

I have already described in detail how to do a beating start in a dinghy. In a yacht the technique is very different, because you can't just pull in the sheets and go: a 12-metre, for example, takes two or three minutes to build up to full speed.

However, in a yacht you do have instruments and you should have a table on board showing how long it takes to go from drifting forwards to full speed in various wind strengths. Armed with this information, approach on port and tack in good time so you have the opportunity to build up full speed. In practice, you'll be lucky if the other boats give you enough room, but make that your aim.

As on a dinghy, I like to take the bearing of the line and calculate the 'square' wind direction. For example, if the line bears 320° then a wind direction of 50° means the line is square. With instruments you can check this constantly, and if necessary start nearer one end. You may also find the table below useful: it shows how many metres you gain with various degrees of bias by being at the favoured end of the line (as opposed to the wrong end), with figures for line lengths of 100, 200 and 300 metres.

Bias	100m	200m	300m
1°	1·7	3·5	5·2
2°	3·5	7	10·5
3°	5·2	10·5	15·7
4°	7	14	21
5°	8·7	17·5	21
6°	10·4	21	31·4
7°	12·2	24·2	36·5
8°	13·9	27·8	41·8
9°	15·6	31·29	46·9
10°	17·4	34·7	52

Line biased so you can just lay the mark from anywhere on the line

In figure 2, going for the no. 1 spot (A) is risky

because there will be a huge bunch by the committee boat and you may have your wind taken or be forced to luff after the start to keep your wind clear. Provided it is a reasonable distance to the first mark, start just to leeward of the bunch (B) with full speed.

Note that you can never say for certain at the start that you *will* lay the mark – the wind may shift or the current may sweep you down. But starting to leeward of the bunch is good if the wind lifts – you will then certainly make it – while if the wind heads you can tack and sail across the fleet on port.

If the current is against you, starting from a little down the line avoids the risk of getting it on your lee bow, being pushed to the right of the committee boat and missing the start line altogether. Only start by the pin (C) when the tide is well under your lee bow and certain to lift you up to the mark.

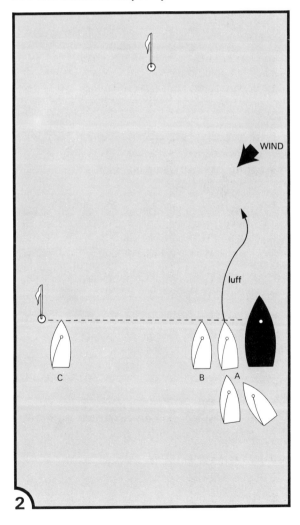

2

You can lay the mark easily, but can only set a spinnaker if you luff first

On a short leg, consider the position of the first mark, for there will be an advantage in sailing the shortest distance to it. The table gives the advantage you gain by starting at the nearest point, as opposed to 100m or more down the line. For example, if the first mark is 500m away and you start 100m from the closest point on the line, you lose 10m on someone who sails the shortest distance.

Distance from Startline to mark	Distance from closest point		
	100m	200m	300m
2000m	2.5m	10m	22m
1500m	3.3m	13·3m	29.7m
1000m	5m	19·8m	44m
500m	10m	38·5m	83m

Next, think about luffing, then setting the kite (figure 3). Ask yourself two questions. Firstly, will you gain speed by luffing (D). Secondly, will you gain speed with the kite (E)? If your answers are yes to both, then the extra distance is probably worthwhile, but you should luff no more than 10° off course. If you aren't going to gain any speed by luffing, then it's not worth deviating from the straight-line course. On a 2000m leg you lose 20m by going up 10° and then down 10°, which is quite a lot to make up.

In a dinghy, it's definitely worth going up if setting the kite will make you plane. But if you're already planing when you're sailing straight for the mark, and luffing will knock you off the plane, forget the luff because the other boats will plane away from you while you're going up and while you're hoisting. You may never get them back. Finally, remember to barber-haul the jibsheet before the start (use the outside genoa track on a yacht) since it makes close reaching much faster.

Beam reach: you can set a spinnaker anywhere on the line

Set the pole early and approach the line on a close reach (F, in figure 4). This gives you good speed and lets you adjust your approach to the line by luffing or bearing away. Don't set the spinnaker until the gun goes. Ideally, you want to start by the committee boat but if there is a huge bunch building up keep down the line a bit: they will inevitably luff and sail a longer distance. After the start sail low – you may have to drop your kite later and point up to the mark, but that should still pay.

If the current is with you, you really should make a timed run. The rest of the fleet won't have a clue, so you should pop out into clear air. Nice feeling isn't it?

Broad reach

As always, do not hoist before the start but do have the pole set ready. In a yacht, the fastest point of sailing is a close reach and that's how you should

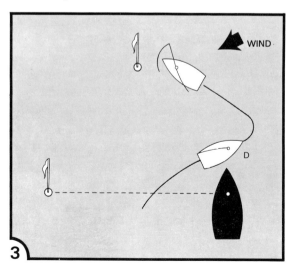

3

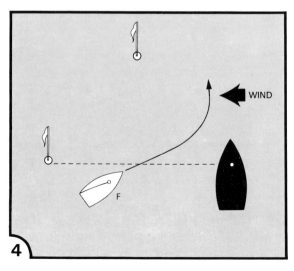

4

approach the line (figure 5). Generate maximum hull speed before you bear away and set, even if that means pulling up the kite late. You will still be going faster than the people who have borne away and hoisted, and that extra half knot can pull you clear of the others. Remember, you always lose a little speed as you hoist.

In a dinghy, acceleration is faster so you simply bear away at the gun, hoist, and go.

Start at the weather end of the line. You can get away with starting at the pin only when the line is long, the distance to the first mark is large and there's a huge bunch by the committee boat. Sail straight to the next mark, and with luck the boats to weather will luff and clear your wind.

Run

With a square line the technique is simple: just reach up and down the line, hoist the pole in good time and, at the gun, bear off and hoist. All other things being equal, start on starboard (figure 6).

It is especially infuriating to have those behind take your wind after a good start. However, you can always gybe out of their windshadows.

Note that, on a square line, provided you have to gybe at least once to get the leeward mark, there is no advantage to be gained by starting at either end. But if the line is not square, you will gain an advantage from the downwind end (X) because you will then be higher on the wind than someone who starts at the other end (Y) (figure 7).

Once again, take a compass bearing down the line, work out what the wind would bear to make the line square and write that on the deck. Constantly watch the wind direction to see how the bias changes.

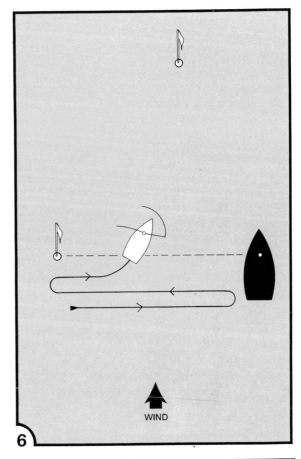

6

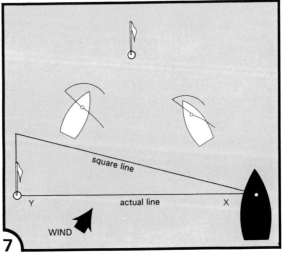

5

7

22 Yacht tactics

Almost all the tactics I've outlined apply to every kind of sailboat. But there are a few that are peculiar to yachts: let's have a look at those next.

Changing sails

There should be no excuse for having the wrong sails up; if your instruments are properly calibrated you should know what to set for the current wind strength and angle.

However, there are always times when you're in doubt, particularly when you're close to a similar boat and you don't want to lose temporarily while you make the change. You may even be undecided as to whether or not to set the spinnaker.

Under these circumstances it usually pays *not* to make the change: I've seen so many times when it has been a mistake. Eventually the competition will make the change and, provided you're ready to follow suit quickly, you won't lose much by waiting to see how he fares. Nine times out of ten you'll sail by, trying not to laugh.

Dipping

Think carefully when you're approaching a starboard-tack boat on port. The difference between just scraping across her bows and ducking her transom is *two* lengths, which in a yacht is a long way.

Have the tactician stand at the back of your boat – after all, that's the bit that has to clear the approaching bows. He then simply watches the competition to see if the bearing of her bow changes. If it gradually drops back, you're clearing. If not, decide whether to duck or tack to lee bow.

If you are going to duck, ease both the main and genoa sheets in good time and try to build up speed – you should be able to gain half a knot. This extra speed will make it harder for him to slam dunk you (tack on you as you dip his stern). Also, try not to use too much rudder as you round his transom as this will only slow the boat.

Being lee-bowed

If the boot's on the other foot and you are on starboard, your main worry is the other boat tacking on your lee bow.

Your only defence is to maximise your speed as you approach: ease the sheets a little early on and foot fast. As he tacks use your speed to luff, then come back on course and try to weather him.

Gybe sets

Assuming the weather mark is to be left to port, the fastest way round is to approach on a reasonably long starboard tack, setting the pole and getting the spinnaker ready. As you round, bear away and hoist (a bear-away hoist).

However, there are a couple of occasions when the much slower gybe set can pay:

1 If you are on a good lift as you approach on starboard: port gybe will take you most directly to the leeward mark.

2 If there is a bunch behind: assuming they stay on starboard, port gybe will take you into clear air.

Below: Approaching the leeward mark on port saves gybing and dropping simultaneously.
Opposite: K747 has judged her crossing to perfection.

23 Yacht racing with electronics

I am indebted to the team at Brookes and Gatehouse, makers of fine yachting instruments, for their help with this chapter.

Almost any piece of electronic kit is now allowed on a racing yacht, not least because of the safety angle. But electronics are mainly used to monitor and improve performance, navigate the boat more efficiently around the course, and to take the guesswork out of strategic decisions. Electronic instruments are also vital for sailing at night, when you can't see the set of the sails anyway. Not bad for a little black box!

The basics

The problem with a large boat is lack of feel: indeed the helmsmen is the only person connected to anything that gives feedback. For the rest of the crew, instrumentation is the only way of seeing how the boat's doing.

A *boatspeed* readout is essential. If you are going fast you can make up for all sorts of errors.

A *windspeed* readout gives the crew a set of markers for sail changes and reefing.

Wind angle helps enormously with sail selection, particularly offwind.

These are all 'inward-looking', and help the crew perform. A *compass* is outward looking: you need one to steer the shortest course and to spot headers and lifts.

With these four pieces of equipment you can start *measuring* your sailing, and look for improvement and repeatability. We will see later that by adding a control unit you can have readouts of true windspeed and direction, VMG and magnetic wind direction. With a polar table programmed into the control unit you can literally race against the computer. And with the whole lot linked to a position finder such as GPS, you can extract tidal data too. Initially, though, let's look at the four basic instruments and see how to use each one.

Boatspeed

A digital readout gives a quicker response and is more precise than an analogue one.

The manual will explain how to calibrate the boatspeed, which is essentially calibrating the log. This involves motoring with engine revs constant over a measured distance, in three directions to compensate for tide. The electronics then take the donkey-work out of the calculation. Lastly, calibrate the instrument so you get equal boatspeed on each tack.

The readout should go in front of the helmsman, with repeaters everywhere so the whole crew can see one and feel involved.

To use the boatspeed indicator watch the readout for a while, so your brain can average the fluctuations. Write down the average. Then change *one* variable, allow the speed to change, and see if it helped. Repeat for all variables – it's perfectly possible to increase the boatspeed by 10 per cent like this. And in any case, never allow the speed to drop without questioning it. I take the view that the boat will do its best speed if it can – it is only the crew that slows it down!

At the end of the day you should make a chart showing maximum boatspeed against various wind strengths and angles. This gives you a target to aim for, especially at the beginning of each leg. (We will see later that VMG gives a better target).

When you tack, have someone call the boatspeed every few seconds. Then you can experiment with gradual and sharp tacks, the objective being not to let the speed drop too far. Having someone call the speed also makes everyone trim faster.

Windspeed

You can't calibrate the windspeed, and the instrument should be accurate from the time it was fitted.

Use it as a force meter. What size of sail do we need? Should we sit out? To weather or to leeward?

When coupled with boatspeed, it gives a clearer idea of targets, such as: "In 10 knots of breeze the boat should be doing 6.6 knots". (We will see later that true windspeed is even more useful).

Wind angle

Calibrating the wind angle indicator entails making sure that the masthead unit is square on top of the mast. So sail upwind on each tack, trimming the same each time, and note any differences. These can be adjusted electronically (so you don't have to climb the mast!)

Wind angle is very useful on the run, in deciding which sail to set and at what angle the pole should be. Upwind the helmsman can begin to correlate optimum boatspeed and pointing angle, though VMG is obviously more accurate.

Electronic compass

It is far more important to go in the right direction than to go the wrong way 0.1 knots faster, so a good compass is essential. Upwind and downwind, constantly check to make sure you are on the favoured tack or gybe, and on a reach check to make sure you are steering the shortest course to the mark. Electronic compasses are so sophisticated that they automatically compensate for deviation if you simply turn the boat through 360 degrees.

Good instrumentation enables the whole crew to monitor performance to get the best out of the boat.

Putting it all together

By using these four instruments *together*, you can get a cascade of information. You *can* do this by using tables – or you can buy a black box to do it for you. Figure 1 shows how the readouts are combined to give more information.

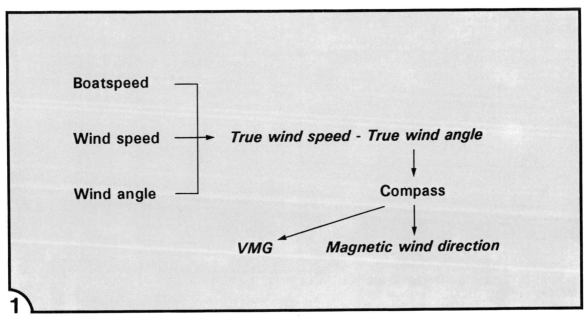

Boatspeed

Wind speed → *True wind speed - True wind angle*

Wind angle

↓

Compass

↙   ↓

VMG   *Magnetic wind direction*

1

Velocity made good (VMG)

VMG is a measure of the progress a boat is making when it is not being steered directly towards its target. It is used mainly on the beat, or on a run when reaching downwind to maximise speed.

In figure 2 A is beating at the optimum angle to the wind. The component of her speed towards her target is x, her VMG. B is pinching and has slowed, so her VMG is reduced to y. C is footing fast but because she is heading so far off-target her VMG is only z.

To use the VMG on a beat:

1 Call up VMG, boatspeed, windspeed, and wind angle on the displays.

2 Steer to a particular wind angle. Maximise the boatspeed at this angle. Note the resulting VMG.

3 Pick a larger wind angle and repeat step 2.

4 If the new VMG is greater, repeat with still larger wind angles until the VMG is maximised.

Make sure you monitor the windspeed throughout: you may be doing better because the wind has increased!

You cannot steer to the VMG readout as you can with boatspeed because it updates too slowly; sadly it is not a 'snapshot' technique. Despite this it is very powerful when used over a period.

Using a computerised 'polar diagram'

Each curve on a polar diagram represents the performance of the boat for a given windstrength. The further a point is from the centre, the greater the boatspeed. If the boat is pointing straight towards her target, the boatspeed is also the VMG. If the boat is beating or running, you can find the VMG by measuring off against the vertical axis.

In figure 3 the windspeed is 10 knots. D is pinching and her VMG is represented by the distance Xm. E is sailing the best course with her VMG maximised at Xn. F is footing too much, with her VMG equal to Xo. G is reaching and her speed is represented by XG. H is steering the best course on a run and her VMG is represented by XP.

An onboard computer can generate a set of 'polar curves' for your particular boat and store them electronically. This gives you a computerised trial horse: the electronics will compare your performance with that of the polar curve and tell you if you are doing 90%, 95% or even 105% of target. This revolutionises night sailing, since you now have something to race against: the computer's VMG when beating or running, and its boatspeed when you are reaching. Note that the computer program does not have to be accurate: you are simply trying to maximise your performance expressed as a percentage of the datum stored in the computer.

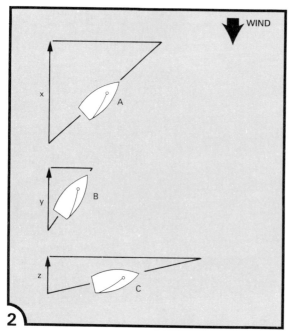

2

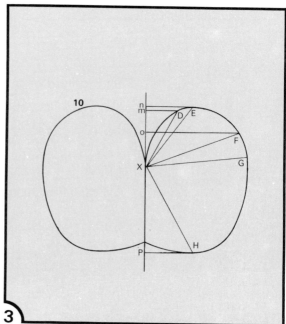

3

If you do not have an onboard computer to do the donkey-work, you can read a figure off the polar tables and race against that.

Using instruments to help with strategy

Magnetic wind direction is brilliant for spotting windshifts. Someone should be noting the readings with time, and building up a pattern to see if the breeze is swinging or oscillating. He might even plot the figures on a graph (figure 4).

Laylines on a beat or run

By comparing the compass course with the magnetic wind direction you can calculate how close to the wind the boat is sailing. You can then calculate the predicted heading on the other tack. Finally, you can sight the mark with a handbearing compass and give the order to tack when the right bearing comes up. Use the same approach to judge a gybe.

Judging a reach or run

Before you get to the next mark enter the magnetic compass bearing of the next leg. The instruments will give you the apparent windspeed and angle so the choice of spinnaker is easy. You can also judge which gybe to take, but do not do a gybe set unless it is favoured by 20 degrees or more. A bear-away set followed by a gybe is usually quicker.

In figure 5, boat J is beating with a heading of 132 degrees. The wind is bearing 090 degrees, so she is sailing at 42 degrees off the wind. She will therefore head 048 degrees on the other tack (90 degrees – 42 degrees) and should tack when the mark bears 048 degrees on the handbearing compass.

Approaching the leeward mark

The electronics will show the favoured tack, and the predicted windspeed. If they are interfaced with a position fixer, such as a GPS set, they will also show the effect of the tide.

Tides and currents

When interfaced with GPS, Decca or Loran the electronics can work out the tidal set and drift. Essentially the black box carries out two calculations:

1 From the compass and log, it works out your movement through the water.

2 From the position fixer, it works out your movement over the land.

The difference is the effect of the tide, plus drift.

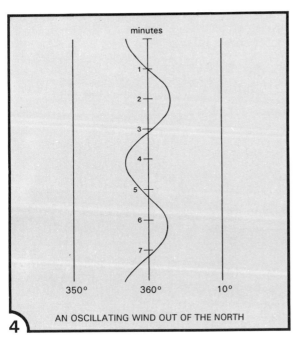

4 AN OSCILLATING WIND OUT OF THE NORTH

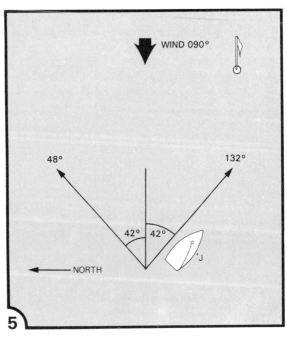

5

24 Match racing

I am indebted to Lawrie Smith, one of the greatest helmsmen in the world, for his help with this chapter.

Match racing makes the adrenalin pump faster than any other branch of our sport. It is a waterborne dogfight to the death between two boats, with no quarter given. If circling the committee boat with a screaming opponent on your tail doesn't make your heart beat faster, all that's left is to try skydiving – without a parachute!

As well as giving raw enjoyment, match racing will also sharpen up your sailing skills and your knowledge of the rules. And it's the only fun way of racing when there are just two boats on the water.

Match racing is now an Olympic sport. The Solings have a normal fleet series and the top boats go through to a match racing series, the winners of which take home the medals. There is also a well-established international match racing circuit, plus, of course, the America's Cup.

What is match racing?

A match is a race between two yachts, usually sailed on course A or B (figure 1). The America's Cup is a special case, sailed on course C. The objective is, naturally, to beat the other yacht over the finish line. Your speed around the course is irrelevant.

Special rules

Most of the normal racing rules apply but they are modified and added to by Appendix 4B. In particular note:

1 A spinnaker may be set without a boom.

2 Before the preparatory signal, a yacht shall keep outside the end of the starting line assigned to her. Within two minutes of the preparatory signal both yachts must cross the start line from the direction of the windward mark (figure 2).

3 Most races have an on-the-water umpire boat with at least two umpires aboard. If you think the other yacht has infringed a rule, shout 'Protest' and fly flag Y from your backstay. The umpire will then fly a green flag (no infringement), or a placard identifying one yacht.

4 The yacht in the wrong then sails clear and does a 270-degree turn, including a gybe. For a penalty before the start, the turn is done after starting. On a windward leg, the turn is done as soon as possible. On a free leg, the turn is done at the beginning of the next windward leg.

5 The umpires may also initiate the penalty (or disqualify a yacht), typically for touching a mark, propelling the boat unfairly or causing damage.

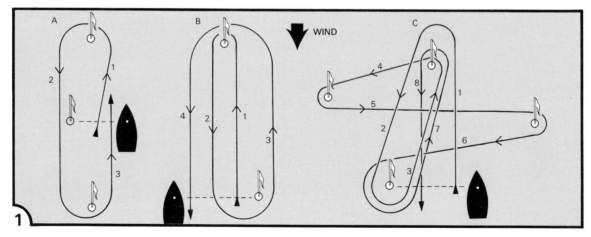

1

Special skills needed

Match racing is about controlling the speed of your boat, and being able to accelerate and decelerate quicker than the opposition.

A favourite tactic is to go head-to-wind and stop the boat as quickly as possible. You will need to do this again and again, so practise! I suggest you slam the boat into the wind, using as much rudder as possible. Go past head-to-wind, holding the jib aback, then come back and hang head-to-wind. (Be careful: as soon as you're past head-to-wind, you're tacking). When you want to go again, back the jib and sail off.

You will also need to circle before the start, trying to catch up with the other boat's transom. It's best to sail an oval course, reaching for a short way to build speed. The bigger the boat, the more important smooth turns are (figure 3).

It is essential to know when you're on the layline both on the beat and the run, so you need to experiment. Draw sight lines on the boat for the wind strength of the day.

What sort of boat gives good match racing?

Ideally you should race in evenly-matched, ponderous boats. 12 metres are perfect, since they weight about 30 tons!

A heavy boat accelerates slowly and turns slowly, so you can't just spin her round and shout "Starboard"! It's easier for the judges to see what's happening when things develop slowly. And it's a better test of helming skill, because it's harder to judge and adjust the speed of a heavy boat. Match racing in dinghies is extremely difficult.

THE START

The pre-start manoeuvring is the most exciting part of the race. Try to keep a cool head, and bear the following general principles in mind.

● *When* you start is irrelevant as long as you start ahead of the competition, or in a better relative position.

● Get on the other boat's transom so you control her.

● If you're defending, stay inside the laylines to the ends of the startline (stay in the shaded area in figure 4). That way, if you get into trouble you can always stop, then get going again and still cross the line.

● If you're attacking, get on the other boat's transom and manoeuvre her outside these laylines. Then when you tack for the line, she will have to follow in your wake.

● Unless there is a significant port bias, start on the

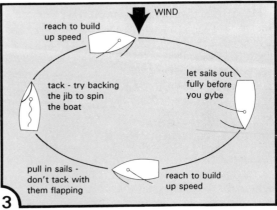

3

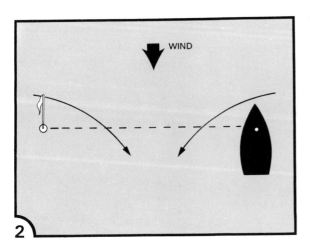

2

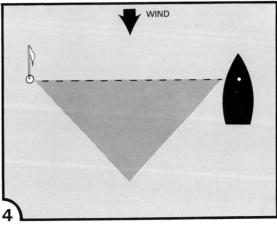

4

other boat's starboard side because she then needs to pull out two lengths before she can tack and cross you.

• The above holds if the line is biased up to five degrees to port. If it's ten degrees to port, start at the port end with as much separation as possible. If the line has a starboard bias, you've *got* to be at the starboard end.

• In the pre-start manoeuvring you never have time to check the line bias, and your instruments will be dizzy. So detail someone to see which way the flags on the committee boat are pointing relative to the line.

Winning start positions with a square line

In figure 5 D is lee-bowing E and will pull ahead.

G is clear of F's lee bow. F will need to pull ahead by two boat lengths before she can tack.

I can sail H on until she is past the pin, then tack for the line first (H can't claim water on the pin). This is a strong position for I because H has to tack or gybe onto port to escape.

Similarly, J can sail K off. But if K gets in a tack she will be on starboard, so J is a little more vulnerable than in the H/I case.

L and M are going to be late for the start, so L will inevitably get there first.

After the preparatory signal

Enough of theory. On with the fray! Before the preparatory signal you must wait outside your designated end of the line. Immediately (within two minutes) after that gun you cross the startline as shown, and lock horns.

There is no proper course before the starting signal so N (figure 6) can initially steer at O. (Eventually N needs to keep straight so O has a chance to avoid her). O should aim to pass N very close, or she will allow N room to start circling before O can begin her turn.

Typically, both boats now start circling with each trying to get on the other's transom.

On her tail . . .

Eventually one boat will catch the other up, and sit on her lee quarter. The pair then head out towards the 'starting' layline (as are P and Q, figure 7).

The lead boat can try to tack to stay inside the

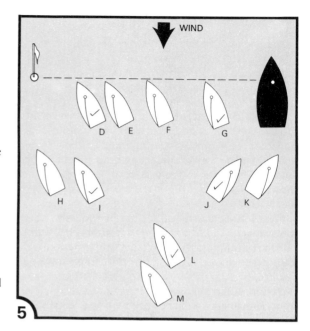

5

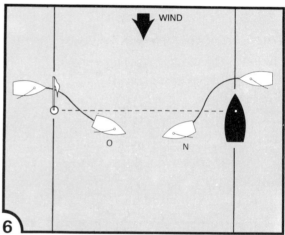

6

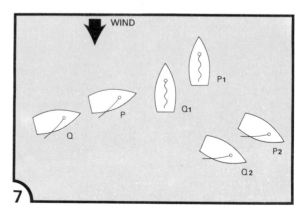

7

layline, but if Q is smart she will luff, then shout "Don't tack in my water" (P1, Q1).

Alternatively P may try to bear away and gybe, but again Q will bear away and shout "Don't gybe in my water" (P2, Q2).

Note that being on port is helpful to P, since if she does manage to tack or gybe she is then on starboard.

How to escape

There are several ways to shake someone off your tail.

1 *Use the committee boat, or the pin buoy.* Head towards, say, the committee boat. As soon as your pursuer is committed to coming the same way as you, do a half circle round the committee boat (you are R or S in figure 8) and sail off in the other direction. Alternatively, carry on round the committee boat and try to get on your rival's tail.

Sometimes the boat following you will take the committee boat the other way (T). In this case just tack (or gybe) once she's committed.

2 *Go head-to-wind suddenly.* This is a standard manoeuvre: slam the boat head-to-wind and stop as quickly as possible. The idea is to get your opponent to slide alongside you (she won't stop as quickly). Hang there: with a bit of luck she'll blow sideways onto you and be penalised (U in figure 9). In the head-to-wind position no-one has the advantage.

Eventually you will be able to back your jib and sail off. Alternatively, if she manages to stay on station (V in figure 9) and if you have sufficient time before the start, simply sail off on a beat. You will soon lee-bow her, pull ahead and be able to tack off.

3 *Keep bearing away.* If your opponent knows what she's doing she will try to stay on your lee quarter, and maintain a reasonable gap. Try to lure her into getting too close; you can then go head-to-wind, slow down (so she slides up your leeward side) and tack (figure 10).

As you bear away there will be a lot of shouting from your opponent about windward boat keeping clear. Remember: she has to give you time and opportunity to do that, and she also has to be close enough to hit you. But she won't want to be that close, or you can escape as detailed above.

4 *Use the spectator boats.* The spectator boats usually assemble well beyond the startline. So if you've got at least three minutes to go, head for

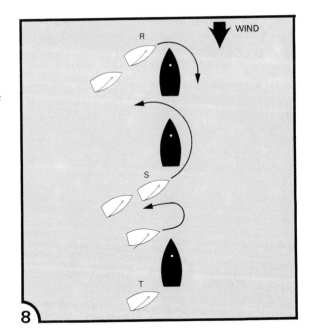

8

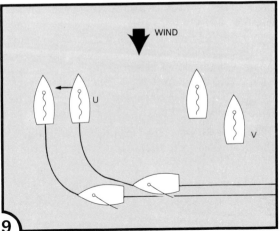

9

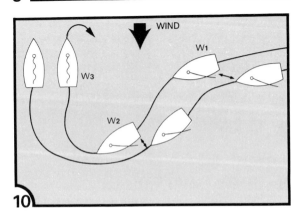

10

them, choose a large stationary boat and then circle round it as you would the committee boat. If you're on the defensive (as we were against *Australia II*) play at the end with the most spectator boats.

5 *Refuse to play!* After the 10-minute gun, broadreach away from the line on port for four minutes. Gybe (onto starboard) and beat back slowly, adjusting your speed to hit the line exactly on the gun.

THE BEAT

After the heat of the start, the beat can come as a welcome relief. Try to settle down and sail fast – and *don't pinch!*

Let's look at a few general principles first.

1 Protect the right-hand side of the course by keeping to starboard of your opponent: that's worth two lengths. The last thing you want is for her to come across on starboard, forcing you to duck. If you are on her left, your objective is to get to the right.

2 Don't forget to watch for windshifts.

3 Although you must cover, remember that the run is coming up; you will need a bit of a lead or you will immediately be blanketed. And if you're slow on the run you may need to take more risks on the beat to give you some breathing space.

4 Think all the time about the laylines. If you're ahead, shepherd your victim towards the nearest layline. If you're behind, stick to the middle.

After an even start

If you are faster (X) carry on until you can tack and cross (figure 11).

If you are going at the same speed (Y) bear away to open the gap, and increase speed. When you're ready, tack and take her transom. Now you're out to the right, which enables you to tack on a shift and come back at her on starboard.

The windward boat can defend by coming with you, trying to sail you out to the layline. What happens then is discussed later.

The first tack

Provided both boats get a good start, and are evenly matched, the race is often decided on the first tack.

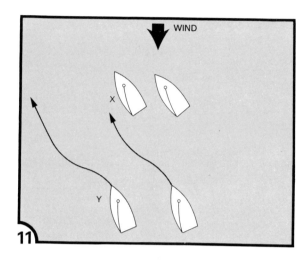

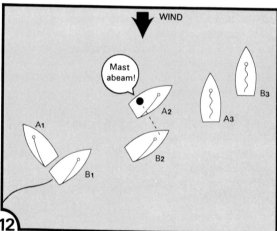

Most of our America's Cup races were decided at this point.

Let's suppose the fun is initiated by B tacking and then ducking A's transom (position 1, figure 12). A must tack immediately, and as the tack is completed call "Mast abeam". I also recommend that A's helmsman waves his arm as he calls, so the judge can see. B can now only luff to close-hauled, and A has a chance of holding her out to the layline. A should then get to the windward mark ahead. During the long port tack A should watch B's jib, which may not back: if it does, shout "Not above close-hauled".

If A is not mast abeam when her first tack is completed, but still hails, B must protest.

If there is no shout, B can luff head-to-wind (position 3). A will drop back into her lee bow, then into the hopeless position and B will be ahead at the windward mark.

A tacking duel

If one boat gets behind, her only chance of avoiding cover is to split tacks.

As soon as it's obvious that you're behind, split tacks immediately. You will need all the time you can salvage to catch up.

The only way to gain is to give something in the short term: do two quick tacks. The leading boat may be tempted not to do the second tack, but to sail on a bit and increase her lead. (Incidentally, this is wrong; the lead boat *must* cover, especially early on. Near the windward mark, cover is not quite so important, because the trailing boat has less chance of a shift). If you get clear air, use it to sail fast and look for a shift. And ideally begin on port, so that after two tacks you're on port again and heading to the right of the course. Look for a shift, so you can tack and come back on starboard at your opponent.

Try not to race yourself out of it – you can't afford to be more than three or four lengths behind on the run, or the other boat will have clear air.

If you're ahead and have got out of synch with the boat behind, tack on windshifts to increase your lead.

In a tacking duel the trailing boat can try a dummy tack. Once again, it's best done on port so you finish up on the starboard side of the course. Warn your crew (quietly!) that a dummy tack may be coming up, push the boat head-to-wind, then fall back onto the original tack.

Meeting on opposite tacks

If you're on port it's difficult to judge whether you can cross the other boat. Send a man aft (it's your transom that has to clear her bow) to keep an eye on the bearing of the opposition. If the bearing changes you should be able to cross her, but if it stays steady you're heading for a collision and will have to duck her transom. (In match racing you need to cross with a good margin, or the other boat may cheat by needlessly bearing away and pretending she had to alter course to avoid you).

All other things being equal you want to cross or duck, rather than tack to lee bow, because your main objective is to get to the right.

Laylines

You must have tacking lines on your boat so you can judge when you're on the layline.

If you're behind, avoid the laylines. Once there, you can't escape from cover because each tack loses you ground. Stay in the middle and initiate a tacking duel.

If you're ahead, shepherd your rival to the nearest layline by applying tight cover if she tacks away from the layline, and loose cover if she sails towards it. Pinch as you approach the layline to open the gap sideways; the decision on when to tack for the mark is then your opponent's. Do not sail over the layline and tack late: the opposition can break cover by reaching off, and still lay the mark. Tack early or on the layline: the other boat will have to sail an extra two lengths to clear her air, and you will need those two lengths on the run. Tacking slightly early is safe: if the wind lifts you will make the mark, while if it heads you will be better off anyway.

THE RUN

The run is a nail-biting experience if you're ahead. Your main objectives are to keep your air clear, and to keep to the left of your opponent. That way she not only has to make up the distance to your transom, but also add another two lengths before she can get across in front of you.

If you're behind, now is your chance to:

● Take her wind.

● Try to get to the left.

● Go off on the opposite gybe (if you're well behind and you reckon she's going the wrong way).

● Slip down to leeward before each gybe so she has to gybe through your wind.

The on-the-water judge in this race is well positioned to spot any misdemeanour.

Choosing which gybe to take from the weather mark

If you are ahead you will normally set off on the favoured gybe, that is, the one on which you point most directly at the leeward mark. But if your opponent goes the other way you'll need to gybe. That way you stay in the same wind as her.

A *bear away set* is quicker, but the danger is that the boat behind will get a puff and will slip below you (figure 13). When you both gybe for the mark, she'll have the overlap.

A *gybe set* is slower but immediately takes you left, which as we've seen is worth two lengths. When you gybe for the mark, like E in figure 13, you'll be unlucky not to have the overlap.

If you're ahead and being covered, sail past the layline before you gybe for the mark. You will then be able to sail in to the buoy on a reach, and it will be easier to keep your wind clear (F in figure 14).

A run to the finish

A match race often finishes on the run. Once again, a gybe set helps because you will be approaching the finish on starboard. That's worth two lengths if she comes across on port to the finish line.

In close-quarters work, note that the pursuing boat has to gybe for the line as soon as she can lay it. The leading boat can protest if she doesn't; otherwise G could sail H on past the committee boat and finish ahead (figure 15).

Rounding the leeward mark

Provided there is no chance of the boat behind getting an overlap, it pays to take the spinnaker down early and stow everything away ready for the inevitable tacking duel.

Don't luff after rounding (unless you have a good lead). The important thing is to be up to speed as she rounds. If you're not, and she tacks immediately, you may stop if you tack to cover.

The last beat

If the finish is on a beat and you're behind, stay in the middle and keep tacking. Once you reach the layline your options are limited.

If you're ahead shepherd your opponent to the layline, then tack for the finish. There is no need to cover her past the layline unless the wind is light and fluky: every tack brings the possibility of a foul-up.

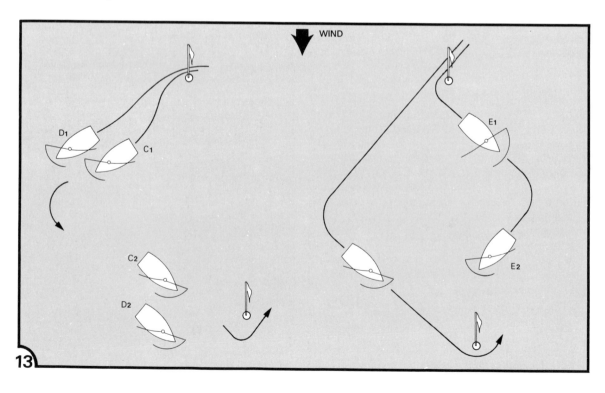

13

Never give up, even when you're well behind. Stay on the opposition's wind – and pray!

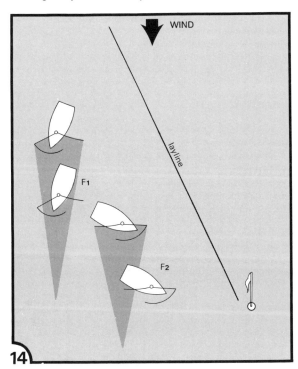

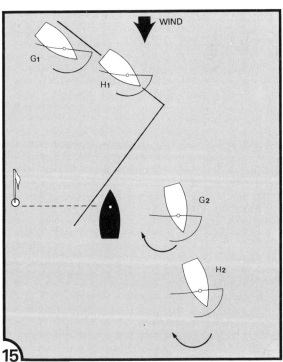

25 Team racing

I would like to thank Will Henderson, who has won the national team championship three times, for writing this chapter.

A team race takes place between two teams, usually with three boats per side. That's what we'll cover here, although it is possible to race with two, four or more boats per side.

What's so special about team racing?

In a fleet race you are concerned with your own position in the fleet, both in the race and in the series. In a team race you are just as concerned with the positions of your team mates as you are with your own, and a winning tactic may well involve you sailing slower, over a longer distance or even being overtaken.

In a fleet race you spend most of your time looking ahead and planning how you are going to improve your position. But in a team race – unless you are in last place – you should be looking behind just as often and thinking about tactics to gain or maintain a winning combination for your team. At the same time you must be alert to attempts by the opposition to execute team tactics against you and your team mates.

Are there special team racing rules?

By and large the normal racing rules apply to team racing, but modified by Appendix 4A (a potted version of which is given below). In fact a variety of scoring and alternative penalty systems are in operation, but I'm restricting this chapter to the system outlined in that appendix.

- You may not interfere with a yacht on a different leg.

- Right of way can be waived between team mates, provided the opposition aren't compromised.

- You can render assistance to your team mates.

- If there is contact between team mates, one

should display a green flag (see below).

- If all the boats are supplied and you have a breakdown, you can fly a red flag (see below) and try to continue. You may get a resail, or your predicted finishing position.

Scoring system

1st = ¾ point
2nd = 2 points
3rd = 3 points
4th = 4 points
5th = 5 points
6th = 6 points

Note that there is a slight advantage to winning, but not much! To see if your team is ahead, add together your places. If the sum is 10 or less, you're winning that race. (Alternatively, if the fleet splits into pairs and you're ahead in two pairs, you're winning.)

Usually there are two races to a match, and the team with the lowest points total wins. (If there's a tie, the team that won the second race is the overall winner.)

Penalties

If you foul another boat you can either fly a red or a green flag.

A red flag means you intend to protest. (As long as you act "reasonably promptly" you are allowed to change your red to a green.) If you are later disqualified in the protest, the committee will add six points to your finishing score. In which case you can only win if your team clocked up first, second and fourth or better.

A green flag means you acknowledge you were in the wrong. 2.5 points are added to your team's score.

My advice is to take a green if you *know* you're in the wrong, especially if your team is in a good position. Protests can go either way, and it's hard to carry six points if you're disqualified.

Note you can fly as many greens or reds as you

like. Note also that if you wilfully hit someone and the collision results in serious damage, your score is loaded by 10 points.

Objectives for each position

Before the race your team should agree on an overall plan for each position. After a while things will happen automatically, but for beginners I recommend taking your agreed plans out in chart form (see the "Sample Tactics" chart). You might also like to make a tidal atlas for each boat, plus a set of tide tables!

Fundamental principles

Now you have an overall plan, but before you put it into action you must become familiar with a few fundamental principles.

1 *Attack before you are attacked.* On a beat, on a reach or at a mark it is easy to slow down an opposition boat behind you so as to let one or more of your team mates overtake you both and thus improve your team position. The opposition can of course do the same to you and your team. It follows that it is nearly always best to attack before you are attacked.

Win or Lose	Our Position	Their Position	Action for our team
Sample Tactics			
W	1,2,3	4,5,6	Sail fast, loose cover
W	1,2,4	3,5,6	Cover 3, convert to 1,2,3
W	1,2,5	3,4,6	Cover 3 & 4, convert to 1,2,3
W	1,2,6	3,4,5	6 sails fast, 1 & 2 loose cover
W	1,3,6	2,4,5	1 covers 2, convert to 1,2,6 and 2,3,4
W	1,4,5	2,3,6	4 & 5 increase distance on 6; if attacked by 2 or 3, 1 must come back immediately to convert to 2,3,4
W	2,3,4	1,5,6	Loose cover 5 & 6, attack 1 if possible
W	2,3,5	1,4,6	Convert to 2,3,4 by covering 4
L	1,4,6	2,3,5	4 covers 5 to convert to 1,4,5. If 2 or 3 attacks 4, 1 must back to convert to 2,3,4
L	1,5,6	2,3,4	1 tries to slow whole fleet until 5 or 6 break through 3 or 4, then convert to 2,3,4
L	2,3,6	1,4,5	2 and 3 cover 4 & 5 to convert to 2,3,4
L	2,4,6	1,3,5	2 covers 3, 4 covers 5 to convert to 2,3,4
L	3,4,5	1,2,6	Try to catch 2
L	3,4,6	1,2,5	Try to catch 2. As soon as this is done attack 5 to convert to 2,3,4
L	3,5,6	1,2,4	3 tries to maintain position or catch 2 while 5 & 6 take on 4
L	4,5,6	1,2,3	Sail as fast as possible – there's always next year!

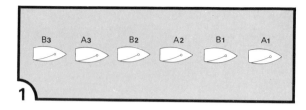

Take a simple example: Team A is winning with a 1, 3, 5 against Team B's 2, 4, 6 (figure 1).

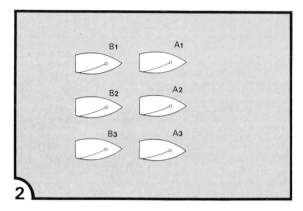

If Team A attacks first, with Team B doing nothing other than to sail as fast as it can in the circumstances, then Team A should improve its position to a 1, 2, 3: A1 slows B1 substantially; A2 slows B2 to a moderate degree and A3 sails as fast as possible (figure 2).

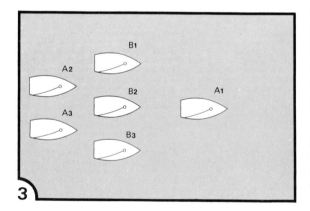

On the other hand if Team A is passive and Team B attacks first, Team B could convert its losing 2, 4, 6 into a winning 2, 3, 4 as follows: B1 slows A2; B2 slows A3 while B3 avoids the cover of A3 and sails as fast as possible (figure 3).

A1 is the first boat home but because she has ignored the needs of her team mates her team has lost. In a good team race, of course, both teams will try to attack and defend at the same time.

2 *Know your scores.* At all times it is vital to know whether your team is winning or losing, and by how much, so that you know what needs to be done to convert a losing combination into a winning one or how many places your team can afford to lose without losing a winning combination. In three-boat team racing simply add up your team's positions, and any score of 10 or less is a winning combination.

The situation gets more complicated when penalty points or retirements are involved, or when the match is a two-race affair. If necessary write down the points from the first race before the start of the second. It is remarkable how difficult it is to do simple additions and subtractions in your head while remembering the answer to an earlier calculation, playing the mainsheet, steering the boat and luffing the opposition. Whenever possible I try to get my crew to keep the score, since he is often in a better position to give the mental arithmetic the concentration needed. This also increases communication between the helmsman and crew and ensures that the crew is as up to date as the helmsman with the race situation.

3 *Beware the unexpected.* Some standard team racing tactics are most unusual in fleet racing. Until you are used to them they can take you by surprise – to the detriment of your boat and your team. One example of this can occur at the windward mark (figure 4). C1 and D1 are approaching the mark close-hauled on port tack some three or four boat lengths ahead of C2. The mark is to be left to port. D1 is overlapped to leeward of C1. In a fleet race D1 would expect C1 to tack onto starboard as soon as she could lay the mark; but in fact C1 sails on well past the layline, carrying D1 with her and allowing C2 to round the mark in front of both of them.

4 *Speed, shifts, bends and velocity gradients.* It is important to remain aware of these as they can help you apply your team racing tactics. However, sometimes you can forget the tactics and use the shifts to break cover and leapfrog up the fleet.

THE START

A good start is just as important in a team race as in a fleet race. However, the definition of a good start is somewhat different. In a team race it doesn't matter whether you and your team mates cross the

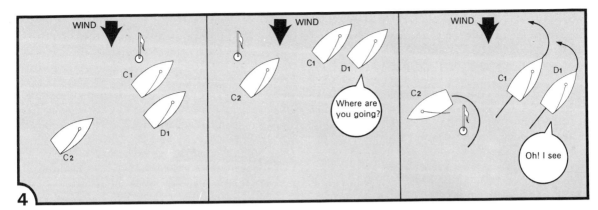

line on the gun or two minutes after it – as long as you cross it ahead of the opposition. Further, in team races the starting line is usually no more than six or eight boat lengths long so being at the favoured end is less important than in a fleet race.

Before the start you and your team mates should have discussed what strategy is appropriate. Have the opposition got any known strengths or weaknesses? If it is the second race of a match can you risk one of the opposition getting away in first place or do you only need to make sure one of them is last? Work it out and tailor your strategy to meet the needs of the situation. If one of the opposition is known to be slow or to be in a slow boat, try to avoid the risk of your faster boats being trapped behind him.

Frequently boats "pair off" and a number of little match races take place before the start. Whether you and your team or any of them should play the start in this way or allow it to be played in this way should depend on the strategic demands of the race. Generally pairing off leads to a fairly even start: if all the pairs return to the start line at different times then at worst you are likely to be 2, 4, 6; at best you will be 1, 3, 5.

On the other hand, should you risk being down in the first two pairs, possibly with your fast boat starting in the last pair a long way behind the first two? The other factor to consider is how good you, your team mates and the opposition are at pre-start match-racing manoeuvres (discussed in detail in the chapter on match racing).

If you or your team want to break up any pre-start match racing you can frequently help each other. In figure 5 E1 sails over to the near stationary F1 and E2 and prevents F1 from bearing away, thus enabling E2 to escape.

In team racing you must be able to sail fast while looking backwards.

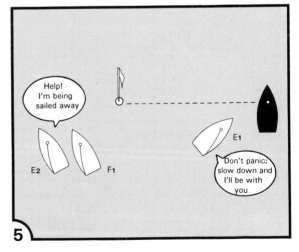

If your team has done very well in the first race of a two-race match, all you may need to do in the second race is keep one of the opposition in last place. In this situation pairing off is a good tactic as it should ensure that at least two of your boats are ahead of one of the opposition.

If the fleet has not broken up before the start and the starting line is reasonably fair, it is usually a good tactic to spread your boats down the line to let at least one of them take advantage of any windshift which comes along and to prevent too much interference between boats in the same team (figure 6).

Many teams arrange the start so that one of their boats starts at or near the windward (right-hand) end of the line and one at or near the leeward end, while the third is a maverick, free to start where she chooses and to harass the opposition. However, your starting tactics must be flexible so your team can take advantage of any opportunities that arise. If the line turns out to be very biased, for example (figure 7), you will want all your boats up at the favoured end.

WINDWARD LEGS

Slowing

When you're ahead you can slow the opposition by interfering with her wind supply: either blanket or lee-bow her (figure 8).

The nearer you are to your opponent the greater the effect you will have. But to stay close to her you will need to slow down yourself, either by letting your sails out (typically the jib only) or by oversheeting them or by a combination of both. In light to moderate winds pulling the boom to windward is very effective (figure 9).

An opponent can also be slowed by luffing, although this will frequently cause her to tack off. You can try to force her to sail a longer or slower course (you could take her the wrong way up a bend or into an area of no wind) but generally it is the boat behind which controls the direction while the boat in front controls the speed.

So, if you are behind on a beat and want to slow an opponent who is in front, you cannot do this directly. But if she is trying to cover, you can slow her very effectively by sailing the wrong way on the shifts and bends or by sailing into an area of lighter wind or stronger adverse current or merely by engaging in a tacking duel. The initial object of this is not to gain a position for yourself (unless you are confident that you can out-tack your opponent) but – assuming that the boat behind is one of your team-mates – it should enable her to overtake and then, if the situation warrants it, come back and help you past your opponent.

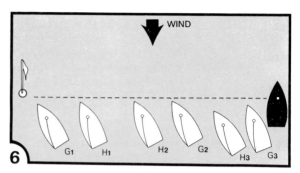

6

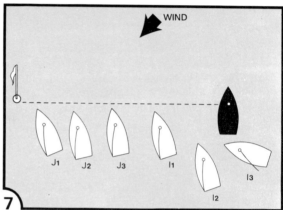

7

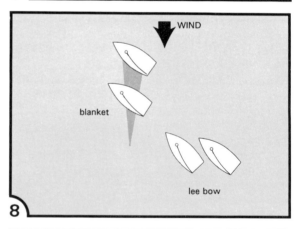

8

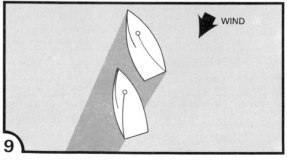

9

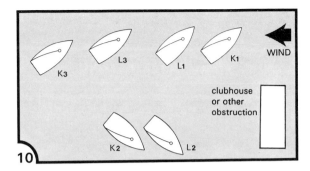

10

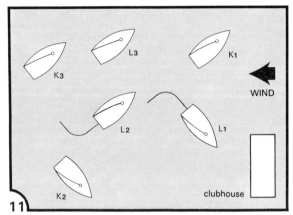

11

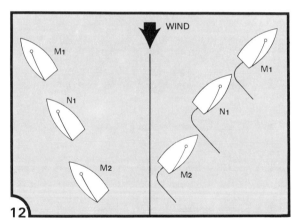

12

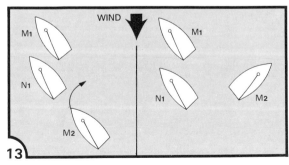

13

For example, in figure 10 Team K initially has 1, 5, 6. By taking L2 into the lee of the clubhouse, K2 lets K3 by. Team K now has 1, 4, 6 and can next convert this to 1, 4, 5.

The counter to this sort of tactic is for L2 to break off from covering her opponent at an appropriate moment and to maintain only loose cover, or preferably for one of her team-mates to maintain the loose cover while she goes the fast way up the beat, thus increasing her distance from her opponent and consolidating her team's position (figure 11).

Bunching

If your team is winning on a windward leg you will want to increase the distance between yourselves and the opposition (see example above). If your team is losing you will want to overtake, but if that is not possible – typically because of effective covering – you want to try and close up the distances. If you are hot on the heels of the opposition as you round the windward mark you will give yourselves the opportunity of overtaking on the downwind legs or at the gybe or leeward marks.

If one of your boats is in the lead while the rest of your team is languishing in fifth and sixth, the leader can slow and bunch the opposition as much as she dares by covering them or by forcing them outside her at marks.

Overlapping the opposition

Sometimes you need to not only slow the opposition, but also force her to go in a particular direction or stop her covering one of your team-mates – otherwise the relative positions of the boats will not change.

So long as N1 covers M2 (figure 12) it does not matter to her that she is also being covered by M1. In order to get her team-mate through, M1 must position herself so that N1 cannot tack when M2 tacks (figure 13).

The smaller and lighter the boat, the more difficult it is for M1 to get into and hold a position where she can prevent N1 from tacking without risking being hit or overtaken. N1 cannot luff above close-hauled, but it is difficult to establish exactly what her close-hauled course is in the disturbed air behind M1. Furthermore there is nothing to prevent N1 from bearing away onto a reach, tempting M1 down with her, and then luffing sharply up to, but not beyond close-hauled (figure 14, overleaf).

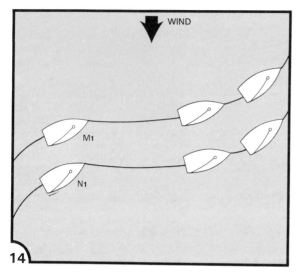

14

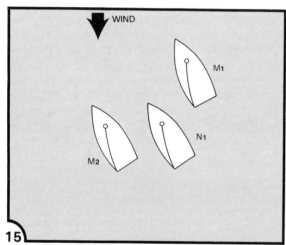

15

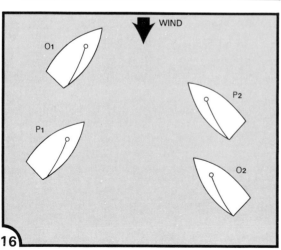

16

Where M2 is also involved a so-called "squeeze" can develop, where N1 is covered by M1 and (eventually) lee-bowed by M2 (figure 15).

It is important that M2 does not bear away onto a reach, since that makes M1's task difficult or impossible. It also delays the whole group and may enable N1's team-mates to overtake and rejoin the fray.

If you are in the position of N1 in the last few examples you will probably want to cover M2 as closely as possible. If you can stop M2 tacking, then even if M1 is stopping you from tacking as well you will not be too concerned, for you will keep the relative positions of the boats the same. In this sort of situation the team which does best will be that which can communicate well and control the speed, position and direction of its boats most accurately and quickly.

The 'pair swap'

This is very satisfying when it works. In our example, Team O is up in one pair and down in the other – in other words Team O has a 1, 4 to P's 2, 3 (figure 16).

Boat O1 increases the distance between herself and P1 so that when the pairs cross, O1 is ahead of P2, and O2 is ahead of P1 (figure 17). The boats in Team O then swap the boats they are covering (figure 18) and sail away up in two pairs – a 1, 3 – which they should quickly convert to a 1, 2 by increasing the distances between themselves and their opponents.

Team P's obvious counter in this case is for P2 to stick close to O2. This would be relatively easy in this example, but more difficult if the pairs are on opposite tacks as they approach (with O1 and P1 on starboard and P2 and O2 on port). P2 then needs to anticipate the situation by calling on O2 for water to pass behind O1, while at the same time maintaining an overlap on O2 to prevent her tacking off and escaping cover.

Team P could also have attempted a pair swap, with P1 taking up the cover of O2 and leaving O1 to attempt a long-range cover on P2. If P1 is quick to put a hard cover on O2, Team P should be able to convert its 2, 4 into a 2, 3. This is a particularly important conversion to effect in a two-boat team race. The team that comes out on top will be the one which anticipates developments and has the boat handling skill to turn every situation to its advantage.

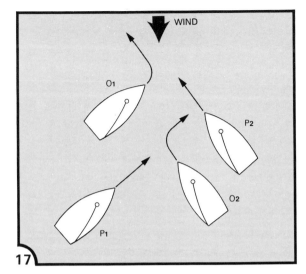

17

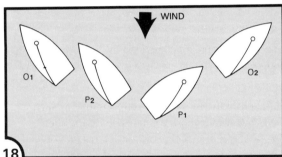

18

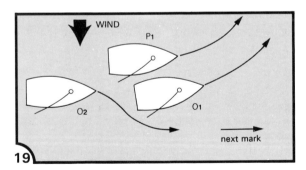

19

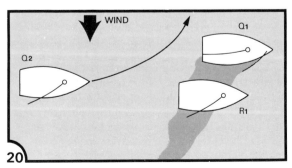

20

Taking a flyer

Unless you are really desperate or very confident, *don't do it.* As long as your whole team remains in touch with the opposition there is still hope, but when one or more of your boats moves out of striking distance your team is doomed.

REACHING TACTICS

Luffing

Luffing is a good way of slowing an opponent to let your team-mate through (figure 19).

The 'reaching tactic'

This makes use of the area of very disturbed wind caused by a stalled mainsail. Trap your opponent to leeward, then pull your main right in. In figure 20, Q1 and R1 slow down while Q2 sails past to windward. It is important that Q1 keeps some way on – at least initially – because if she slows down too much R1's momentum may carry her through the lee of Q1 and into clear air, leaving Q1 looking very stupid. In dinghies, a boat in Q1's position would keep her way on by making sure her jib keeps drawing.

There is a risk of R1 breaking through if the wind heads at the critical moment and she catches the new wind around the front of Q1. Assuming this does not happen, R1's normal counter-tactic is to slow down and prevent herself obtaining an overlap on Q1 so that she can keep Q2 behind her (figure 21). If Q2 goes to windward R1 can luff; if Q2 goes to leeward she will find no wind and stop. It is not uncommon for the whole fleet to pile up on a reach with each boat trying to sail more slowly than the one in front so as to keep her tactical options open.

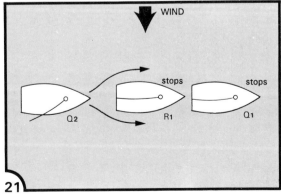

21

THE RUN

The run gives a losing team its best opportunity to break through, since it has control of the wind supply (figure 22).

The leading team's defensive weapons are speed and the power to luff, but if the boats are closely bunched it will be difficult to maintain a 1, 2, 3. If possible the members of the leading team should put some distance between themselves and their opponents before getting onto the run to reduce any wind-shadowing effects.

In some circumstances it may be worth sacrificing yourself or one of your team-mates. For example, if you are in a one-race match and leading 1, 2, 3 with only the run and a short beat to go, you could afford to sacrifice 3 to make 1 and 2 safe (figure 23).

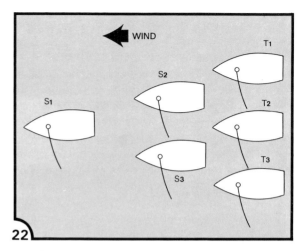

Tactics at marks

In certain situations one boat will wish to close up the fleet. This might occur where one team has a 1, 5, 6. The closer the fleet is bunched together, the greater the chances of 5 or 6 breaking through into 3 or 4. In these circumstances if 1 slows down or stops at each mark she can force the opposition to sail around and outside her. Provided she accelerates soon enough, she will not lose first place but she will bunch the fleet (figure 24).

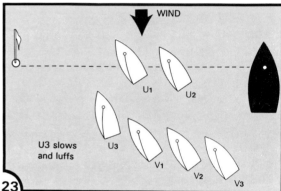

The finish

There is no point in hovering within a few metres of the finishing line in the hope of executing some last-minute tactic – you will probably foul up. Sail away from the finish towards your victim to give yourself the time and space to carry out the manoeuvre.

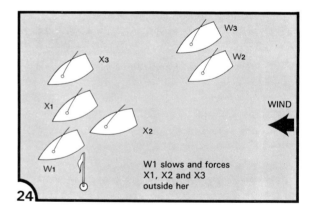

Bigger or smaller teams

If you have more (or less) than three boats per team the tactics are much the same, but there are a few variations.

In a two-boat-per-side match the boats tend to pair off more than in a three-boat event, and they can take a very long time to get around the course because the only safe winning combination is a 1, 2.

A four-boat team race is often arranged with a points scoring system which penalises the last boat rather than favouring the first boat. If this is not the case, then any team that gets a 1, 2 will win, regardless of the positions of the third and fourth boats in the team (work it out!).

Racing with five or more boats per team obviously gives scope for more winning and losing combinations than with fewer boats. Perhaps because of this, and because such races are relatively unusual, there tends to be a greater emphasis on speed. Despite this, there is no reason why you cannot employ all the team tactics discussed.

Other books in the Sail to Win series

Sails   *John Heyes*
It is vital to get your sails right. This handbook shows you how to work with your sailmaker to develop sails which match your rig, and then how to set them properly.

Dinghy Helming   *Lawrie Smith*
One of Britain's top helmsmen gives specific advice on maximising boatspeed in all conditions, plus helming skills required during the race itself.

Dinghy Crewing   *Julian Brooke-Houghton*
Crewing a modern racing dinghy is a complex and demanding task. Olympic medallist Julian Brooke-Houghton explains the skills required and shows how helmsman and crew work together as a race-winning team.

Wind Strategy   *David Houghton*
Most 'sailing weather' books are too large-scale to be relevant to racing on inland or coastal waters. This book shows how to predict the wind over the racecourse area, during the time-span of the race, using simple 'rules of thumb'.

Tuning Your Dinghy   *Lawrie Smith*
A logical, systematic approach to setting up a racing dinghy and fine-tuning it on all points of sailing. Plus a 'trouble shooting' section to pinpoint and cure specific weaknesses in the boat's performance.

The Rules in Practice   *Bryan Willis*
It is a popular fallacy among racing sailors that you need to know the rules. You *do* need to know your rights and obligations on the water – the rules can always be looked up afterwards. International rules experts Bryan Willis looks at the key situations that repeatedly occur on championship courses, from the viewpoint of each helmsman in turn, and summarises what you may, must or cannot do.

Tides and Currents   *David Arnold*
How tides can help you win races – whether inshore, offshore or on an Olympic triangle.

Boatspeed – Supercharging your hull, foils and gear   *Rodney Pattisson*
Written by an Olympic Gold Medallist, this book gives the secrets of achieving a really fast boat – whether new or second-hand – plus detailed information on choosing and installing all the control systems.

The Winning Mind – Strategies for successful sailing   *John Whitmore*
Ninety per cent of sailing takes place from the neck up, yet most books concentrate on the hardware and on technique. *The Winning Mind* will not only help the sailor to perform better and more consistently but also help him and his crew enjoy their sailing to the full. Equally useful to the casual fair-weather sailor or the Olympic racer.

Also published by Fernhurst Books

Sailing the Mirror   *Roy Partridge*
Mirror Racing   *Guy Wilkins*
Topper Sailing   *John Caig*
The Laser Book   *Tim Davison*
Laser Racing   *Ed Baird*
Racing Crew   *Malcolm McKeag*
Racing Skipper   *Robin Aisher*
Tuning Yachts and Small Keelboats   *Lawrie Smith*
Boardsailing: a beginner's manual   *John Heath*
Board Racing   *Geoff Turner & Tim Davison*
The Catamaran Book   *Brian Phipps*
Knots & Splices   *Jeff Toghill*